"Prof. Austin Sarat and his co-authors have produced a powerful indictment of state execution by lethal injection. I urge anyone interested in criminal justice, constitutional values, and in abolishing the death penalty to invest the time in reading and acting upon this important work."

—U.S. Senator Chris Coons, D-Delaware and Member, Senate Judiciary Committee

"This book offers compelling evidence that the promise of lethal injection is a hollow one. Sarat's illuminating account shows that the situation is getting worse as states employ secrecy and obfuscation to hide their experimentation with different drugs and methods. An essential contribution."

—Stephen B. Bright, former Director of the Southern Center for Human Rights

"Austin Sarat's trailblazing scholarship about lethal injection makes it impossible for anyone to claim that it's a humane form of killing. This conscience-stirring book documents the skyrocketing of botched executions. It is a reminder of what a great teacher Sarat is."

—Lincoln Caplan, Senior Research Scholar, Yale Law School

"Sarat has followed the brute rituals of the death penalty in the United States for years and nowhere as powerfully as in this grim book, a cry of the heart and mind for yet another look at the botched executions inflicted by the state and the barbaric accommodations made by the courts. An exceptional, searing, and scrupulous history of ghastly murder that also gives a voice to those sacrificed on the altar of legal vengeance."

—Colin Dayan, author of *The Law Is a White Dog*

LETHAL INJECTION AND
THE FALSE PROMISE OF
HUMANE EXECUTION

LETHAL INJECTION AND THE FALSE PROMISE OF HUMANE EXECUTION

AUSTIN SARAT
with
Mattea Denney,
Greene Ko,
Nicolas Graber-Mitchell,
Rose Mroczka,
Lauren Pelosi

stanford briefs
An Imprint of Stanford University Press
Stanford, California

Stanford University Press
Stanford, California

Printed in the United States of America on acid-free, archival-quality paper

Library of Congress Cataloging-in-Publication Data available on request.

Library of Congress Control Number: 2022935885

ISBN: 9-781-5036-3353-7 (paper)
ISBN: 9-781-5036-3451-0 (ebook)

Cover design: Rob Ehle
Cover art: Shutterstock

Typeset by Classic Typography in 11/15 Adobe Garamond

CONTENTS

Will posterity shudder at a model of a gallows set up in complete working order on a shelf, as we of to-day shudder when we examine the ancient instruments of torture collected in the World museums? Will the American of the year of Our Lord 2,000 be so far in advance of us? We venture to hope so.

—Elbridge Gerry, Alfred Southwick, and Matthew Hale, *Report of the Commission to Investigate and Report the Most Humane and Practical Method of Carrying into Effect the Sentence of Death in Capital Cases* (1888, 36)

The science that serves to kill so many could at least serve to kill decently. An anesthetic that would allow the condemned man to slip from sleep to death (which would be left within his reach for at least a day so that he could use it freely and would be administered to him in another form if he were unwilling or weak of will) would assure his elimination, if you insist, but would put a little decency into what is at present but a sordid and obscene exhibition.

—Albert Camus, *Reflections on the Guillotine* (1963, 179)

How enviable a quiet death by lethal injection.

—Justice Antonin Scalia, *Callins v. Collins* (1994, 1141)

As long as the United States continues to use capital punishment, scholars and commentators on public affairs should continue to write about it and highlight the damage it does to this country and its values. Even though the number of people caught up in the death penalty system is small in comparison with the numbers in jails and prisons, there is something deeply troubling about a society that kills any of its citizens no matter what they have allegedly done. That sense of trouble and its accompanying unease has drawn one of us (Austin) to this subject for a large part of his career.

But it is never clear how to approach this task in a way that feels right. We study and write about offenders, victims, and the families of both whose lives are shattered and ended by crime and punishment from a privileged distance. Research and writing in themselves cannot bridge that distance. Nothing really can.

But research and writing about the death penalty can bear witness to the killing that the state uses as criminal punishment. It helps memorialize that grim act. In doing the research for, and writing, this book we felt a strong sense of obligation to those whose lives were inevitably part of the lethal injection story. Throughout that often troubling process we also were sustained by the hope that this kind of documentary project could play a part in naming and understanding what scholars have called "law's violence."

We decided to include photographs of some of the those whose executions we describe to give a human face to our subject and remind us of the real people and lives lost in the killing state. That seemed like the least we could do. All of these photos are disturbing, but readers may find one of them, a post-execution picture of Doyle Hamm, particularly so. We hope that it can help us understand what the state does in all of our names.

LETHAL INJECTION AND THE FALSE PROMISE OF HUMANE EXECUTION

1 ONE WEEK IN THE WORLD OF LETHAL INJECTION

In April 2017, with its supply of lethal injection drugs about to expire and with thirty-two inmates still on its death row,[1] the state of Arkansas announced that it would perform eight executions over an eleven-day period. Though legal problems ultimately halted half of them, four were carried out as originally planned. They were all conducted with a cocktail of lethal drugs that Arkansas had never before employed.

Before this execution spree, Arkansas's last execution had been in 2005. For that execution, the state used the well-established, "traditional" three-drug lethal injection cocktail: sodium thiopental, pancuronium bromide, and potassium chloride. But the state failed to replenish its supply of those three drugs in the years that followed, and, in 2013, when Arkansas tried to buy more, it found those drugs were no longer available. This led the state to devise a new drug protocol. The protocol it came up with, however, which called for the use of lorazepam and phenobarbital,[2] was quickly criticized. Critics noted that not only had those drugs never before been used in an execution, they were also unlikely to cause death quickly, if at all.[3] By 2015, the state was forced to retreat, deciding this time to adopt another three-drug cocktail that was actively being used by other states: a sedative named midazolam was to be injected at the start of the execution, followed by two other drugs—vecuronium bromide and potassium chloride.[4]

Despite Arkansas's efforts to find what it hoped would be an effective drug cocktail for lethal injections, the executions it conducted in 2017 had deeply troubling results. In many ways, the story of what happened when Arkansas went ahead with this new drug cocktail tells, in condensed form, the story of lethal injection's recent history in the United States. Once touted as a technological miracle that would ensure executions would be safe, reliable, and humane, since 2010 efforts by states across the country to use lethal injection for execution have, as this book describes, been beset by one problem after another. These repeated problems, mishaps, and failures, like the ones that occurred in Arkansas, show the hollowness of that hope and call into question the viability of America's continuing attachment to the death penalty. Despite these long-standing problems with lethal injection, over the last decade death penalty states including Arkansas have clung fast to this method of execution, rather than abandoning it. They have revised and repaired it as best they could to keep the machinery of death running, even as new problems emerged with each revision and repair.

The four executions that Arkansas went ahead with in 2017 were carried out during a single week in mid-April. Its first execution, and its first ever using the drug midazolam, was that of Ledell Lee. Lee had been sentenced to death for the 1993 rape and murder of his twenty-six-year-old neighbor, Debra Reese. He had been tried twice. During his first trial, several people testified in support of Lee's alibi. That trial had ended in a hung jury. At his second trial, however, the defense inexplicably called no alibi witnesses. This time, the jury found Lee guilty and sentenced him to death.[5]

Several civil rights organizations tried to stop the execution, contending that insufficient efforts had been made to avoid the possibility of convicting an innocent man. On the eve of Lee's execution, the Innocence Project—an organization which works to overturn wrongful convictions—and the American Civil Liberties Union (ACLU) brought a last-minute appeal to the Arkansas Supreme Court, specifically noting that DNA evidence from the crime scene had never been tested with the most modern technology. The court, however, refused to stay Lee's execution, arguing that this last-minute appeal came too close to the scheduled execution date. The execution proceeded on April 20, ten days before Arkansas's batch of new lethal injection drugs would expire.

FIGURE I. Ledell Lee. (*Source:* AP.)

Lee's execution, which appeared to state officials to cause less pain and suffering for him than they had feared it would, led the state to believe it had found a drug cocktail that would be reliably both lethal and pain-free. After placing intravenous lines (IVs) in Lee's arms, the execution team started the flow of the sedative midazolam at 11:44 p.m.[6] As it entered his body, Lee's eyes slowly shut and he began to swallow repeatedly, an effect that commonly occurs when midazolam is used in an execution. Once it had been administered, the execution team began the flow of vecuronium bromide and potassium chloride. The coroner pronounced him dead twelve minutes after the execution began.

Although many problems had been documented when midazolam was used in executions in other states, officials contended that Lee's execution had gone off without a problem.[7] Four days later, Arkansas went ahead with its plan to kill a second man—a man named Jack Jones. Jones's execution, however, like two other executions that week, revealed the unpredictability of lethal injection.

In 1996, Jack Jones was sentenced to death for murdering a woman named Mary Phillips. On a June night in 1995, Jones broke into an accountant's office in Bald Knob, Arkansas. There, he found Mary Phillips and her eleven-year-old daughter, Lacy. After attempting to rob Mary, Jones bound her to a chair, raped her, and strangled her with a cord. Jones then assaulted Lacy, strangling her and crushing her skull.[8]

When investigators arrived, they found Lacy in a closet tied to an office chair.[9] Miraculously, she survived and was able to testify at her assailant's trial. There was little doubt about Jones's guilt. When the police first questioned him, he waived his Miranda rights and confessed to the crime.[10]

As a child, Jones had been subject to physical abuse by his father, who regularly beat him, and had also suffered "sexual abuse at the hands of three strangers who abducted and raped him."[11] By 1994, Jones was a suicidal thirty-year-old with bipolar disorder, depression, and ADHD. But during his sentencing, the jury found that aggravating factors, including the cruelty of his crime and a previous criminal record, outweighed mitigating factors like his troubled childhood. They sentenced him to death.

A little more than two decades after his conviction, guards steered the wheelchair-bound Jack Jones into Arkansas's death chamber.[12] When the witnesses arrived at 7:00 p.m., Jones was already strapped to a gurney with intravenous lines sticking out of his arms. At 7:06 p.m., the warden wiped a hand over his face, signaling the execution's start.[13]

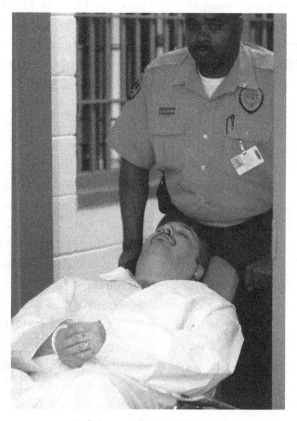

FIGURE 2. Jack Jones. (*Source:* AP.)

Throughout the fourteen-minute execution, correctional staff checked Jones's consciousness by sticking a tongue depressor in his mouth, "lifting his eyelids and rubbing his sternum."[14] According to Jones's lawyer, his client began to gasp and gulp for air four minutes into the execution—a sign that he was experiencing physical pain. He added that Jones's mouth moved like a "fish... chomping on bait."[15] Soon, that movement slowed, and the team declared Jones dead at 7:20 p.m.

Lawyers for Marcel Williams, whose execution was scheduled for later that night, and state officials offered different interpretations of Jones's mouth movements. Williams's lawyers called his death "torturous," contending that Jones "was moving his lips and gulping for air [which is] evidence that the [midazolam] did not properly sedate him."[16] A Department of Corrections spokesperson disagreed, however, stating that, "the inmate was apologizing to the department director, Wendy Kelley, and thanking her for the way she treated him."[17] As part of Arkansas's standard procedure, before the lethal drugs started to flow, the prison staff shut off the death chamber microphone,[18] so it is not possible to resolve which of these interpretations is more accurate.

But whether or not Jones had been dying a painful and prolonged death, was gasping for breath, or was "thanking the department director," there were other problems prior to the execution itself, including officials' error-ridden attempts to place an IV in Jones's veins. Although Arkansas claimed in a final report that it only took eight minutes to place Jones's IV, Williams's attorneys said it actually took forty-five minutes to find a suitable vein.[19] Moreover, as is often the case when such difficulties occur, the official's report did not mention the many failed attempts to find such a vein. Yet the autopsy report noted that medical examiners "found five needle marks on Jones's neck and clavicle... area" and that the needle marks had been covered up with makeup.[20]

Botched lethal injections, like Jones's, are a continuing and problematic part of the story of capital punishment in the United States.[21] From the beginning of the republic, execution practices have been designed to differentiate law's violence from violence outside the law—to sharply set capital punishment apart from the crimes the law condemns. This country has sought ways of killing that would neither allow the condemned to become an object of pity nor to appropriate the status of the victim. Lethal injection was once thought to represent the fulfillment of this distinctly American quest.

The search for a humane way to put someone to death today contrasts markedly with the execution practices of other eras and other places. As historian and social theorist Michel Foucault notes, in the past executions were "more than an act of justice"; they were a "manifestation of force."[22] They were always centrally about the display of the majestic, awesome power of the sovereign to decide who suffers and who goes free, who lives and who dies. Selecting the method to kill was the sovereign's prerogative. But execution methods were usually chosen for their ability to convey the ferocity of the sovereign's vengeance. They were designed to make the state's dealings in death majestically visible to all and to create fearful, obedient subjects. Live, but live by the grace of the sovereign; live, but remember that your life belongs to the state. These were the messages of European executions in earlier eras.

Today, execution in the United States has been transformed from dramatic spectacle to what is supposed to be a cool, bureaucratic operation, and the role of the public is now strictly limited and controlled. Modern executions are carried out behind prison walls in what amounts to semi-private, sacrificial ceremonies in which only a few selected witnesses are gathered to see and, in their seeing, to sanctify the state's taking of the life of one of its citizens.[23]

America's death penalty has been inextricably tied to the instruments used to carry it out. From hanging to electrocution and the firing squad, from electrocution to lethal gas, from electricity and gas to lethal injection, the United States has moved—though not uniformly across states—from one technology to another.[24] The legitimacy of capital punishment depends in part on the reliability of execution methods. In the United States, these methods have been chosen with the goal of masking the condemned person's physical pain while allowing citizens to imagine that putting someone to death is clean, efficient, and painless.[25] For more than fifty years, among the options available, people have argued that lethal injection is the method most likely to achieve these goals and that it puts people to death quietly, invisibly, and humanely. These arguments have proven to be highly persuasive, and today, lethal injection is this country's primary execution method.[26]

With the invention of new technologies for killing or, more precisely, with each new application of technology to killing, political leaders and judges have proclaimed previous methods barbaric, or simply archaic, and have tried to put an end to the spectacle of botched executions. As a federal district court once noted in a decision upholding the constitutionality of lethal injection: "There is general agreement that lethal injection is at present the most humane type of execution available and is far preferable to the sometimes barbaric means employed in the past."[27]

The court's use of the word *humane* is but one among many occasions on which this word has been associated with lethal injection. But it has turned out to be a double-edged sword. It has signaled the hope of its proponents, but, at the same time, it has served as a linguistic disguise that has let the government do what it wants when it puts someone to death.

The belief that lethal injection has the capacity to move the condemned from life to death swiftly and painlessly—to ensure that execution is nothing more than "the mere extinguishment of life"[28]—remains widely held today. In 2014, a Gallup poll found that 65 percent of the respondents said lethal injection is the most humane method of execution used in the United States.[29] But executions like Jones's disrupt that idea and suggest that, like the other methods of execution used since the start of the twentieth century, lethal injection is far from fool-proof in assuring the law's violence does not turn cruel.[30]

That reality was again brought home the same day Arkansas executed Jack Jones when it also put Marcel Williams to death. It was the first time since 1999 that a state executed two people in a single day.[31] Williams had been sentenced for the 1997 kidnapping, rape, and murder of Stacy Errickson, a twenty-two-year-old mother of two.[32] The Williams execution lasted seventeen minutes, and media witnesses could not tell when officials administered each drug. His lawyers said that he continued to move "up until three minutes before he was declared dead."[33] Jacob Rosenberg, one of the reporters at the Williams execution, described the bodily movements that occurred during the time before Williams was finally declared dead. "His eyes began to droop and eventually close... His breaths became deep and heavy. His back arched off the gurney [countless times] as he sucked in air."[34]

Throughout the execution, state officials were unable to tell whether the drugs were actually killing Williams, and they conducted consciousness checks by feeling his pulse and touching his eyes. After one check, a member of the execution team could be seen whispering "I'm not sure."[35] Williams's lawyer made a statement to the press after the completion of the execution where he said he was "gravely concerned" about what had taken place and that he feared Williams had been both conscious and in pain during the procedure.[36]

FIGURE 3. Marcel Williams. (*Source:* Jessi Turnure.)

Both Jack Jones's and Marcel Williams's executions were troubling. But an even more troubling execution took place three days later when Kenneth Williams was put to death in Arkansas's fourth and final killing of the week. Williams was sentenced to death in 2000 for multiple killings. In 1998, he kidnapped and killed a college cheerleader, Dominique Hurd. After spending less than a year in prison, Williams "escaped by hiding in a hog slop-filled tank of a garbage truck."[37] Once outside the prison, he shot a former warden, stole his truck, and led police on a high-speech chase during which he hit and killed another man. Like so many others who commit such crimes, Williams grew up in an abusive household.[38] By the time he was nine years old, he had joined a street gang and was later sexually abused.[39] According to testimony at his clemency hearing, he decided to become "the predator, not the prey" at a young age.[40] In August 2000, he was sentenced to death for his new crimes.[41]

After spending nearly seventeen years on death row, on April 27, 2017, Williams became the 200th person, and the 140th Black man, executed in Arkansas since 1913.[42] As was the case with Marcel Williams, Kenneth Williams's execution by lethal injection was not painless or swift and instead involved extensive physical agony and evidence of suffocation. About three minutes after receiving a dose of midazolam, Williams began to thrash about and convulse on the gurney. One reporter said that he "lurched forward fifteen times, then another five times, more slowly" before gasping and taking labored breaths.[43] Witnesses could hear the inmate moaning and groaning.

Despite those widely reported details, state officials insisted that everything went as planned, calling the execution "flawless." A Department of Corrections spokesperson said that "Williams [only] coughed without sound—in direct contradiction of media witness testimony."[44] Governor Asa Hutchinson refused to heed calls for an investigation and reportedly "remained confident in the state's protocol."[45]

However, an independent autopsy confirmed that Williams's execution was anything but flawless. Joseph Cohen, a pathologist who conducted the postmortem, concluded that Williams "experienced pain" and likely felt "a sensation of air hunger, fear, shortness of breath, respiratory distress, and dizziness."[46] The press and Williams's legal team described his execution as a "horrifying" botch.[47]

Even as the state encountered mishaps during its week-long execution spree, Arkansas did not slow down. Instead,

FIGURE 4. Kenneth Williams. (*Source:* AP.)

it used various maneuvers allowed by its execution protocol—such as inserting the IV behind a curtain and switching off the microphone after an inmate's final words—to obscure key parts of the execution process from view. Against considerable evidence to the contrary, the state insisted that every execution went according to plan. And more than three years later, a federal court said that Arkansas could continue using midazolam in executions if the state tweaked its procedures slightly.[48]

This single week in Arkansas in the spring of 2017 provides a brief, but representative, glimpse into lethal injection's recent troubles. In every lethal injection during the more than thirty years between 1977 (the year Oklahoma become the first state to adopt the method) and 2009, death penalty states used only a single lethal injection protocol. However, drug shortages and other problems beginning in 2009 forced those states to make a choice: they could halt capital punishment, revive defunct methods of execution, or try new ways of carrying out lethal injection. Most states chose the third option, a choice that forced them to turn to untested drugs and drug combinations.

With the implementation of these drug combinations over the last decade, however, new problems have emerged. No longer does lethal injection signify a single thing with a standard drug combination. Today, different states use a wide variety of drugs and procedures. As these varied lethal injection protocols and drugs have proliferated, executions have become more error-prone and unpredictable such that an already unreliable execution method has become even more problematic.

Adding to its problems is the fact that lethal injection executions generally have been carried out by people with no training in the various tasks that such executions require. Many of those whose job it is to set IV lines and administer the drugs have no idea what they are doing. As one member of an execution team in California said, "Training? We don't have training, really."[49] It is frequently the case that for team members, "the day of the execution is 'the first time...in their life they have picked up a syringe... so it's a little stressful for them to be doing this.'"[50]

The result, as Professor Eric Berger notes, is that "the list of mistakes that states have made is astounding."[51] That list includes misunderstanding the way lethal injection drugs work, difficulties setting IV lines in inmates' veins, inaccurately assessing whether an inmate is unconscious or not, and choosing unsafe or contaminated drugs or ones not allowed under the governing regulations. Lethal injection, once thought of as a model of efficiency in the grim business of state killing, is now a method marked by mishaps and mayhem.

While scholars and journalists have argued about the complicated ethical and legal issues associated with capital punishment, this book is the first to focus exclusively on the promises and problems of lethal injection itself. It describes how and why this execution method became widely accepted in the United States and the new problems that emerged with it in the decade between 2010 and 2020. The book brings to light data on lethal injection protocols that have not been previously available and discusses mishaps that occurred during that ten-year period. It tells a story of bureaucratic maneuvering, adaptation, and cover-up as death penalty states adopted secrecy statutes and adjusted their protocols to make it harder to identify and observe lethal injection's flaws. It also explains why claims about the "humaneness" of lethal injection, marshalled by those who order and carry out executions, persist even as changes in the last decade have made the practice, already unscientific, even more chaotic, unaccountable, and inhumane.[52]

The story of lethal injection in the United States is riddled with state secrecy and deception, public experimentation on the human body, and utterly gruesome spectacles. Arkansas's unnerving week of executions in 2017 is but one episode of a larger and frequently disturbing history. That history can be traced to practices of capital punishment brought to the United States by its European colonizers[1] and antedates the Declaration of Independence and the Constitution.

The first recorded execution in the colonies took place in 1608 when Captain George Kendall was put to death in Jamestown, Virginia. Kendall, a member of the original Jamestown council, faced the firing squad for allegedly spying for Spain.[2] Throughout American history, treason would continue to be punishable by death, but the lack of legal specificity in the colonies about what kind of crimes warranted capital punishment led to the creation of new legal statutes regarding the death penalty in the aftermath of Kendall's execution. Four years later, in 1612, Virginia Governor Sir Thomas Dale proposed the Divine, Moral, and Martial Laws, which prescribed the death penalty for offenses such as stealing grapes, killing chickens, and trading with Native Americans.[3] Since that time, the legal, moral, and divine justifications for capital punishment have been hotly debated.

From the time the Constitution and Bill of Rights were ratified in the eighteenth century, the United States has tried to reconcile its use of capital punishment with the Constitution's Eighth Amendment, which prohibits the use of "cruel and unusual punishment."[4] It has invested faith in science to achieve this goal and, like Dorothy in Oz, followed a technological yellow-brick road. This quest and this faith have led death penalty states to use several different execution methods—shooting, hanging, electrocuting, gassing, and lethal drugs—each of which was, at one time or another, held out as the gold standard in state killing.[5]

For the first one hundred years of its existence, the most popular method of state execution in the United States was hanging. Between 1776 and the end of the nineteenth century, the condemned regularly were marched to the gallows. With a noose slipped around their necks, they fell to their death suspended from a tree or a wooden scaffold. They were supposed to die via the "hangman's fracture"—a break in the second vertebrae that would cause instantaneous death. But sometime during the mid-nineteenth century, opinions about the "cruelty" of hanging began to change.

Newspapers were rife with graphic descriptions of horribly botched state hangings. In some of those cases, the condemned were suspended just above the ground for up to twenty minutes, writhing and gasping for air. Others suffered full or partial decapitations. One well-publicized, gruesome hanging occurred in California in January 1888 when Nathan B. Sutton was executed for fatally shooting Alexander Martin. With the swing of a trap door, Sutton dropped almost five feet. The rope's force tore open his neck, spewing blood upward into the air.[6] The crowd of over two hundred collectively cried out in horror. Sutton hung for fifteen minutes before dying.[7]

In the years prior to Sutton's execution, state governments around the country had already started looking for new ways of conducting executions. New York lawmakers, for example, publicly acknowledged their fear that such horrific botched hangings would either produce public sympathy for criminals who were condemned to death or fan bloodthirstiness among New Yorkers.[8] Unless the state found a less gruesome execution method than hanging, New York's leaders feared that their constituents might develop a "taste" for violence. They also worried that gruesome executions blurred the line between state and criminal violence. The slow strangulations and bloody decapitations experienced on the gallows "resemble[d] the revolting" crimes for which inmates were punished.[9]

If the state continued to conduct inhumane executions—and newspapers continued to cover them—state officials worried that the death penalty's legitimacy would be jeopardized.[10] In 1886, New York Governor David Bennett Hill responded to such concerns by appointing a commission to find a new, more efficient, and less painful mechanism of state killing.[11] It was during this search that lethal injection would be considered for the first time as a way to put people to death in the United States.

Before the development of anesthetics during the Civil War, the commission's quest would have seemed futile. Pain, not just on the gallows, was an inescapable fact of life and death in the United States.[12] Those who endured injuries and illnesses would suffer, as little therapeutic relief was possible.[13] Medical science did not put much stock in the alleviation of pain.[14] However, the development of sedatives in nineteenth-century surgical suites changed the way in which people in this country thought about pain. Now, the pain wrought by both minor and mortal injuries could be quelled by morphine or sulfuric acid. As the political scientist Timothy Kaufman-Osborn has noted, "middle-class" sensibilities were offended by needless suffering, and large segments of the public came to believe that pain should be avoided whenever possible, even for someone like Nathan Sutton.[15]

Motivated by these developments, the commission Governor Hill appointed was launched in the hope of finding an execution method that the public would stomach.[16] The group was chaired by Elbridge Thomas Gerry, a prominent New York lawyer and social reformer who had founded the state's Society for the Prevention of Cruelty to Children.[17] Gerry led the commission through a systematic examination of execution methods as diverse as the guillotine and the garrote. They eventually narrowed their consideration to two methods: the electric chair and lethal injection,[18] both of which were considered cutting-edge technological innovations that might enable the kind of "humane" execution that state leaders believed other forms of execution could not ensure.

In the late 1880s, the electric chair had only just been invented by a New York dentist named Alfred P. Southwick. As the commission envisioned it, the electric chair would be a simple wooden chair with a headrest, footrest, metal plate, and electrode.[19] Support for it stemmed from its perceived humanity, simplicity, and affordability.[20] Its proponents claimed that it would not cause any "prolonged agony for the condemned." The flash of an electric spark would instantly kill the inmate, taking only one five-hundredth of a second.[21]

But opponents on the commission argued that electricity would be no more humane than hanging. Electricity was unpredictable, they said; the amount of current needed to kill an inmate would depend upon how the electricity was applied and upon the "constitution" of the subject. It was impossible to know if the chair would kill inmates instantly.[22] Opponents also pointed out that electricians feared that the chair would "damage the prestige of the electrical industry" and hurt electric companies financially.[23] Yet most of the commissioners preferred the electric chair to hanging even as they considered yet another alternative—death by lethal injection.[24]

DEBATING THE CRUELTY OR HUMANITY OF LETHAL INJECTION

When New York's Gerry Commission seriously enter-
tained using lethal injection as a method for state executions, it was the first public body in the United States ever
to do so. However, lethal injection as a method of execution was not itself new, and its origins can be traced to
Germany during the seventeenth century when the earliest iterations of the hypodermic needle were developed.[25]
Yet, it was not until the 1850s that a refined design, along
with a newfound understanding of anesthetics, brought
the needle into widespread use.[26] With this development,
the injection of drugs became a primary means of treating
common maladies and anesthetizing patients during surgery. However, there was also a broad public fear of this
new medical technology, and while injectable drugs eased
many people's suffering, the hypodermic needle was also
linked to gruesome, painful deaths.[27]

During the nineteenth century, the pages of newspapers
in the United States were plastered with horror stories
about these injections' dangers. Wedged between syndi-
cated columns and high society gossip were graphic
descriptions of morphine overdoses and deadly science
experiments, all of which were wrought by a deadly combination of drugs and hypodermic needles. This new technology—which promised to end needless suffering during
medical procedures—also possessed a lethal potential.

By 1886, legislators across the United States were taking notice of this deadly potential, and lethal injection

made the New York state commission's shortlist to replace hanging. Use of this technology was first proposed to the commission by Julius Mount Bleyer, a New York doctor.[28] He invited the commissioners to envision that "the condemned could be executed on his bed in his cell with a 6-gram injection of sulfate of morphine."[29]

FIGURE 5. Julius Mount Bleyer. (*Source:* WikiMedia.)

The arguments for and against lethal injection were very similar to those made about the electric chair. Proponents touted its humanity. They argued that, if done correctly, the procedure would be painless. The inmate would be asleep "within thirty minutes, the condemned man's heart would stop and he would be dead."[30] In addition, pro-lethal injection commissioners said that unlike hanging, the method could not be botched; if the inmate was not responding to the drug, officials could simply inject them with more of it.[31] The procedure's perceived simplicity and low risk of complication led some to believe that a prison warden could quickly learn how to administer an injection.[32] And it would be cheap. All that was needed was a needle and a small amount of morphine.[33]

In sum, the proponents argued, lethal injections would be undramatic and private events that would stem both public sympathy for criminals and bloodthirstiness. Rather than creating a spectacle, lethal injection would produce a death like falling asleep.[34] It offered a way for the state to distinguish its punitive violence from criminal violence and appease members of the public who were troubled by hanging's brutality.

On the other hand, lethal injection's opponents feared that the method would actually be easily botched—especially if doctors did not conduct the procedure.[35] For inmates who never used drugs, they said, the "sudden" injection of a poison could result in a "violent" death. For those who regularly used drugs, a high tolerance for morphine would result in a slow death. In other words, some commissioners thought that lethal injection would not be more humane than hanging.

But lethal injection's opponents made a second argument: lethal injection, they said, would be too humane. Although this argument clearly contradicted the first—which said that the method could result in an inhumane or slow death—it nevertheless proved effective. Opponents claimed that if lethal injection worked as the proponents claimed it would, then it would take the dread out of death and would dampen capital punishment's deterrent effect.[36]

Ultimately, lethal injection's opponents on the commission prevailed. But their success cannot really be attributed to the strength of their arguments, which were mired in a complex logic. Instead, lethal injection failed to be adopted in 1888 because of an external factor: the medical community took an unwavering stance against it. Doctors "did not want the syringe, which was associated with the alleviation of human suffering, to become an instrument of death."[37] While pushback from electricians did not tarnish the commission's view of the electric chair, the medical community's concerns made lethal injection a nonstarter. The commission rejected it and opted for the electric chair.

For most of the next century, electrocution would be an execution method of choice in many parts of the United States. It would also become a powerful symbol of the death penalty itself. But innovation and experimentation with ways of putting people to death did not stop. In 1922, those efforts led Nevada to replace hanging with the gas chamber rather than electrocution, and other states soon followed suit. Those two "modern" technologies accounted for almost all executions until the last quarter of the twentieth century when a series of gruesome botched electrocutions and gassings initiated yet another search for a way to execute humanely.

That search revived interest in lethal injection. But for nearly a hundred years after New York's decision, no state in the United States authorized that method of execution. The early legislative debate over electrocution and lethal injection—dominated by arguments about lethal injection's humanity and cost—foreshadowed how this debate would unfold almost a century later in Oklahoma when two state legislators pushed for yet another change in this country's execution arsenal and this time sought an alternative to electrocution and the gas chamber. They led the charge for lethal injection and succeeded in doing what lethal injection's proponents had failed to do in New York.

TWENTIETH-CENTURY REFORM OF CAPITAL PUNISHMENT AND THE BIRTH OF LETHAL INJECTION

For much of the twentieth century, states had wide discretion to determine when a person should be sentenced to death. This discretion, however, led to significant inconsistency in the criteria juries used to apply the death penalty.[38] Because of this, in 1972, the Supreme Court effectively placed a moratorium on the death penalty in the United States, ruling in *Furman v. Georgia* that the death penalty was, in fact, cruel and unusual punishment as then administered. It therefore contravened both the Eighth and Fourteenth Amendments because of the vast discretion states' death penalty statutes gave juries during sentencing.[39]

After the Supreme Court handed down its ruling in *Furman* and blocked executions nationwide, the State of Georgia responded by passing a new death penalty statute. Its statute required the jury to weigh aggravating and mitigating evidence and instructed appellate courts to consider death's proportionality in each case.[40] This new law was intended to enable the state to recommence executions in a way that accommodated the Supreme Court's ruling in *Furman*. Its legality, however, would quickly be put to the test.

In 1973, Troy Gregg and a traveling companion, Floyd Allen, were hitchhiking in Florida and picked up by Fred Simmons and Bob Moore. The next morning the bodies of Simmons and Moore were discovered in a ditch nearby.[41] Gregg admitted to shooting then robbing Simmons and Moore. After Gregg was convicted of murder and sentenced to death under the new Georgia statute, he appealed, citing *Furman,* and claimed that the death penalty violated the Eighth Amendment. The landmark case, known as *Gregg v. Georgia*, made its way to the Supreme Court where the court ultimately held that Georgia's new death penalty statute was in fact constitutional and thus ended the de facto moratorium on the death penalty in the

United States.[42] As Justice John Paul Stevens put it, "We now hold that the punishment of death does not invariably violate the Constitution."[43] *Gregg* gave a green light to states which wanted to get on with state killing. All they had to do was reauthorize the death penalty with the new procedures that the court had approved.

Oklahoma was quick to do so. The same month as the *Gregg* decision was announced, Oklahoma's first-term Democratic Governor, David Boren, convened a special legislative session to restore capital punishment.[44] At the time, the state used the electric chair as its method of execution. However, its only electric chair was no longer in working condition.[45] The Oklahoma Director of Corrections, Ned Benton, estimated that fixing it would cost $62,000, and the Oklahoma legislature began to look for a cheaper alternative. It briefly considered using lethal gas but, after realizing that building a gas chamber would cost the state at least $200,000, turned its attention elsewhere.

Two legislators, State Senator Bill Dawson and State Representative Bill Wiseman proposed that the state adopt an entirely new method of execution: lethal injection. Dawson, a Democrat, previously had worked as a lawyer, Methodist minister, college professor, and auctioneer. Subsequently he served nine years in the Oklahoma State Senate and later three years on the Oklahoma Corporation Commission.[46] Wiseman was a Republican from Tulsa, Oklahoma, who had been raised as a Quaker. He would later say that he decided to promote lethal injection to ease his conscience for his previous vote to restore Oklahoma's death penalty.[47]

Dawson and Wiseman's proposal mirrored arguments made by lethal injection's supporters on the Gerry Commission almost a century prior. They argued that it had two clear advantages over other methods. First, it was much cheaper than most other ways of putting people to death, including electrocution, lethal gas, hanging, or shooting.[48] Second, they contended that it would be much more humane. Because no execution in any country had ever been carried out by lethal injection, they had no evidence on which to base this claim. Nonetheless, they declared executions using this method could be accomplished with "no struggle, no stench, no pain."[49]

Dawson and Wiseman weren't sure how to draft the legislation authorizing lethal injection and describing how it would kill. They needed advice—What drugs should be used? And how should they be administered?—so they reached out to the Oklahoma Medical Association. However, the association quickly turned them away; aiding the legislators, it contended, would violate medical ethics.[50]

Undaunted, the pair went from one medical practitioner to another seeking help imagining what lethal injections should look like in the United States. They were repeatedly rebuked. Ultimately, however, A. Jay Chapman agreed to work with them. Chapman was the state's chief medical examiner. He believed that lethal injection would be less violent and gruesome than the electric chair.[51] However, Chapman conceded that he was "an expert in dead bodies but not an expert in getting them that way."[52]

FIGURE 6. A. Jay Chapman. (*Source:* AP.)

Chapman offered a blueprint for Oklahoma's lethal injection law: "An intravenous saline drip shall be started in the prisoner's arm, into which shall be introduced a lethal injection consisting of an ultrashort-acting barbiturate in combination with a chemical paralytic."[53] When asked why he selected a combination of an anesthetic and paralytic agent, Chapman admitted that "he didn't do any research" and "just knew from having been placed under anesthesia [himself] what [the execution] needed."[54] Although Chapman was neither an anesthesiologist nor a toxicologist, the Oklahoma statute ultimately copied his proposal almost word-for-word and helped make it the model for almost all lethal injection statutes in the states that reinstated the death penalty after *Gregg*.[55]

The proposal to adopt lethal injection was quite controversial among death penalty supporters in Oklahoma.

Old arguments were revived. In an interview with a local newspaper, E. L. Keller, a Republican state senator, commented that lethal injection would give murderers "the easiest way out."[56] Others said that it would prompt suicidal people to commit murders in hopes of dying painlessly at the hands of the state.[57] Some opponents imagined that convicts would intentionally build up immunity to lethal injection drugs to prevent their deaths, and others contended that children would become afraid of intravenous injections. A few of lethal injection's opponents questioned the premise that this new execution method was indeed more humane than other methods. However, Democratic State Senator Gene Stipe—one of Oklahoma's "powerful and colorful politicians"—offered an amendment to limit the duration of lethal injections.[58] Senator Stipe argued that if there was no such limit, the condemned might languish between life and death for hours or even days. Stipe proposed a five-minute limit, erroneously claiming that the longest recorded hanging in United States history lasted four minutes and fifty-eight seconds and that no electrocution exceeded five minutes. As he put it, "If this is supposed to be something humane, and supposed to be something better, then we better put a time limit on how long they can put this thing in your vein! They could have a guy lie there all day!"[59] In response, Dawson commented that Chapman anticipated most lethal injections would be over in a "matter of a few minutes." After a short discussion, the amendment failed.

Others argued that the promise of lethal injection would prove illusory since there was no humane way to take a human life. Democratic State Senator Bob Funston said,

I came to this chamber today intending to vote for this bill. And I don't know exactly why I was going to, but I'm not going to now. And I guess the basic problem that I had, that I thought I could cleanse from my conscience by voting for this bill, was the question of whether there is a humane way to take a human life. And I'm not really sure, when you basically get down to it, that there is a humane way to ever take a human life.[60]

However, for the majority of the state senators, Chapman's testimony on the bill was sufficient to convince them of the method's humanity—or perhaps they simply weighed cost considerations more heavily.

The Senate passed the lethal injection bill by a 26-20 vote. The House quickly followed suit, 74-18. On May 11, 1977, Governor David Boren signed the legislation, making Oklahoma the first state to adopt lethal injection as its method of execution. The law called for the use of only two drugs: an "ultrashort-acting barbiturate" that would anesthetize the inmate and a "chemical paralytic" that would asphyxiate the inmate. The specific drugs—sodium thiopental and pancuronium bromide—would not be chosen until four years later. Although the original law only called for two drugs, after sodium thiopental and pancuronium bromide were selected, a third drug was also added—potassium chloride. Together, these three drugs would make up what became the "standard" three-drug, lethal injection protocol.[61]

Chapman once again was behind the selection of drugs included in the protocol, and he again let his hunches and conjectures drive his decisions. He later claimed that even though a combination of an anesthetic and a paralytic agent guaranteed death, he added a third drug because he "just wanted to make sure the prisoner was dead at the end."[62] The decision to use potassium chloride as the third drug was also quite arbitrary. Chapman admitted that he "didn't do any research," and he said he relied solely on the fact that "it's just common knowledge" that potassium chloride is lethal.[63]

THE DIFFUSION OF THE LETHAL INJECTION

Despite the unscientific, almost random, origins of Oklahoma's lethal injection protocol, it "put Oklahoma in one of those rare instances of being a pioneer"[64]—a win for Dawson and Wiseman. However, Oklahoma was not too far ahead of the pack. At the same time that its bill was being debated, Texas's legislature was considering a similar lethal injection proposal.

In Texas, lethal injection's proponents emphasized that the method would be a less violent alternative to electrocution. Republican Texas Representative George Robert Close described the use of the electric chair as "a very scary thing to see. Blood squirts out of the nose. The eyeballs pop out. The body almost virtually catches fire. I voted for a more humane treatment because death is pretty final. That's enough of a penalty."[65] W. J. Estelle, the director of Texas's Department of Corrections, said that "the lethal injection method suits our state of civilization more than electrocution."[66]

Texas's most ardent death penalty champions, such as Democratic Representative T. H. McDonald, called lethal injection a "slap on the hand" and questioned whether potential criminals would fear the death penalty if they knew that they would receive painless deaths.[67] Others echoed McDonald and questioned whether "drug injection is going to deter a would-be murderer from doing it" when it provides "an easy escape hatch" for murderers who "have been on drugs before...[and] won't mind taking another drug injection."[68]

Death penalty abolitionists also objected to Texas's lethal injection bill, arguing that capital punishment was always inhumane and cruel, regardless of the method used. They were concerned that switching to lethal injection, which better masks signs of violence and pain, would "salve the public conscience" and open an execution floodgate.[69] Pointing to the fact that Black inmates were much more likely to get the death penalty for similar crimes than their White counterparts, critics added that the apparent humanity of lethal injection would not benefit most of the condemned. Instead it could help "the affluent white majority which kills blacks, browns and poor 'white n—' in the name of Texas."[70]

As the lethal injection bill made its way to the governor's desk, death penalty abolition groups organized public demonstrations. They had testified at legislative hearings urging the state to halt all executions rather than adopting a new way of killing. In one instance, members of Citizens United to Rehabilitate Errants (CURE), a prisoner support and prison reform organization founded by Charles James and Pauline Sullivan in San Antonio, packed a House committee hearing on death penalty proposals wearing black armbands and "thou shall not kill" buttons.[71]

Nonetheless, on May 12, 1977, Texas became the second state to adopt lethal injection, just one day after Oklahoma. Its statute was almost identical to Oklahoma's but did not name specific drugs.[72] After spending several months considering various drugs and drug combinations, the Texas Department of Corrections decided to use "sodium thiopental in lethal doses."[73] And, like Oklahoma, Texas added pancuronium bromide and potassium chloride before carrying out the first lethal injection in U.S. history in 1982.

After Oklahoma and Texas, several states rushed to change their execution method to lethal injection without waiting to learn the results of its early adoption. They acted on the basis of its promise rather than experience with it in Oklahoma or Texas. Before Texas put lethal injection to its first test, Idaho, New Mexico, and Washington also adopted it.[74] In doing so, these early adopting states mostly copied, or paraphrased in their legislation or execution protocols, the Oklahoma statute's language mandating that "death must be inflicted by continuous, intravenous lethal administration of a lethal quantity of an ultra-short acting barbiturate or other similar drug in combination with a chemical paralytic to cause death."[75]

Idaho issued its new execution guideline in 1978. Its language varied only slightly from Oklahoma's and stated that "punishment by death will be inflicted by continuous intravenous administration of a lethal quantity of an ultra-short acting barbiturate in combination with a chemical paralytic agent until death is pronounced by a licensed physician."[76] When New Mexico passed its lethal injection bill the next year, its legislation again repeated the wording of Oklahoma's statute that drew on Chapman's suggestions, calling for "a continuous, intravenous injection of a lethal quantity of an ultrashort-acting barbiturate in combination with a chemical paralytic agent."[77]

Between 1976—the year the Supreme Court reauthorized the death penalty in *Gregg v. Georgia*—and 2020, Oklahoma and Texas executed a combined total of 681 inmates. The number of executions these two states carried out by lethal injection far outpaced the other three early adopter states that executed only a combined total of nine inmates over the same time period.[78] Two of the three early-adopters—New Mexico and Washington—have since abolished the death penalty, and Idaho has carried out only three executions since it adopted lethal injection.[79] In those states the choice of lethal injection was a compromise between supporters and opponents of the death penalty that allowed for the death penalty's revival but with a supposedly humane execution method.

The very first execution in the United States using lethal injection took place on December 7, 1982, when Texas executed Charles Brooks, Jr. at its Huntsville state penitentiary for his role in the 1976 murder of a twenty-six-year-old car mechanic named David Gregory.[80]

FIGURE 7. Charles Brooks, Jr. (*Source:* Fort Worth Star-Telegram Collection, Special Collections, University of Texas at Arlington Libraries.)

As he awaited execution, Brooks had been led to believe that lethal injection would produce a calm and painless death. His lawyer described how Brooks "thought that there was nothing to fear in death by injection. He believed that he could set it up to be like the surgery after the first of his bullet wounds." "I remember the first time," Brooks said, "I fought the, it was, I think it was ether. I remember fighting it, I was trying to make myself stay awake, you know. They put a mask over my face, and I was trying to make myself stay awake. And it was like— I can still remember it, fuzzy like—...But anyway, it just seemed like it had a soothing effect.'"[81]

But this first lethal injection was neither soothing nor painless. In fact, it eerily mirrored the first electrocution in the United States. That electrocution, which was horribly botched, took place in New York State in August 1890 when William Kemmler was put to death for the hatchet murder of his common-law wife, Matilda "Tillie" Ziegler.[82] Like Kemmler's electrocution, Brooks's lethal injection also did not deliver a quick and humane death.[83]

The morning before Brooks's execution, Dr. Ralph Gray, the medical director of Texan prisons, examined his veins. Dr. Gray told the *New York Times* that he thought the inmate had "plenty of good veins" that could support an IV. Yet, during the execution, three technicians repeatedly failed in their efforts to insert an IV into a vein in Brooks's arm—splattering blood onto the sheet covering his body.[84] During the several minutes it took for the drugs to take effect, Brooks looked forward in terror. He wagged his head, his fingers trembled, he mouthed words, and let out a harsh rasp.[85]

Dick Reavis, a journalist with Texas Monthly, made an agreement with Brooks in the weeks leading up to his execution date. When Brooks was injected, he would shake his head back and forth if he suffered any pain. As the execution proceeded, Brooks slowly turned his head from one side to the other and then up and back to one side.[86] It took seven minutes for him to die.

Brooks's execution gained considerable attention in states that were then considering reinstating the death penalty and switching to lethal injection, but it did not deter them from doing so. Most notably, in Massachusetts where voters approved a state constitutional amendment by referendum (54 to 35 percent) authorizing capital punishment and where lethal injection was already under consideration, newspapers dedicated special sections to covering the Brooks execution.[87] Yet Massachusetts proponents of lethal injection rehashed arguments like those used in Oklahoma and Texas, promising, in spite of what happened to Brooks, that lethal injection would provide inmates a painless and humane death. In an interview with the *Boston Globe,* the lethal injection bill's sponsor, Republican State Senator Edward P. Kirby, called Brooks's death a "successful execution" and commented that "technology has come a long way since the electric chair... and because an injection is less painful and less offensive, it would be foolish not to use it."[88]

Opponents of lethal injection in Massachusetts questioned whether it indeed guaranteed quick or painless death and pointed out its stigmatizing effect on doctors and the medical profession. Local groups, such as Physicians Against the Death Penalty, and physicians such as Dr. Jonathan Welsbuch, a former director of the Massachusetts prison health system, objected to using "medical knowledge to kill someone."[89]

Others opposed the bill to reinstate capital punishment and introduce lethal injection on moral grounds. Alan D. Sisitsky, a Democratic state senator from Springfield, Massachusetts, argued that "with a life sentence we can make corrections, with the death penalty we cannot."[90] Democratic State Senator Patricia McGovern pointed out the unfairness of the death penalty stating that "the Claus von Bülows of this world will never die under this bill, only the poor will die."[91]

Nonetheless, one week after Brooks's execution, Massachusetts became the sixth state to adopt lethal injection, once again prescribing the drug cocktail created in Oklahoma and first used in Texas. Within a year, seven additional states—Arkansas, Illinois, Montana, Nevada, New Jersey, North Carolina, and Utah—had switched their execution method to lethal injection.[92] Each continued to rely on Oklahoma's original lethal injection formula. Arkansas, for example, required a "continuous, intravenous injection of a lethal quantity of an ultrashort-acting barbiturate in combination with a chemical paralytic agent until the defendant's death is pronounced according to accepted standards of medical practice."[93] Many state lethal injection statutes also followed Oklahoma's decision to allow its Department of Corrections to decide drug dosages and required only that a "lethal dose" or "lethal quantity" of drugs be used in executions.

As other states began to consider lethal injection, they turned to Texas for advice and expertise. Lawmakers and correctional officials from around the country made pilgrimages to the Huntsville Penitentiary, which housed that state's execution chamber, and consulted with Texas officials as they drafted legislation and developed their own protocols. For example, when Wyoming adopted lethal injection in 1984, corrections officials traveled to Huntsville to meet its warden, Jack Pursley, and attended an execution seminar.[94] A former Wyoming corrections official acknowledged that "Wyoming's injection procedure is cloned from the Texas injection procedure." He also added that he was "confident that Wyoming's policy based upon proven Texas procedures will be reliable."[95] Colorado adopted lethal injection the same year, and Gene Atherton, a former warden of Colorado State Penitentiary, explained that its corrections officials visited Texas and Oklahoma and copied their protocols because they "seemed time-honored, tested, well-designed and effective."[96]

As Louisiana, which adopted lethal injection in 1990, developed its protocol, officials collected sample protocols from fourteen states including Texas. However, because most of them were brief and omitted important details, they went to Huntsville to learn about the drugs used in executions: "how they are administered, in what amount, and by whom."[97] To their surprise, the warden of the Huntsville facility—after refusing to discuss the details over the phone and later checking to ensure that the visitors from Louisiana were not recording their in-person conversation—bluntly stated that "he didn't really have so much of a policy about [lethal injection]... as they just did whatever worked at the time."[98] He told his visitors that he "wasn't totally concerned about the amounts [of drugs] or what it may or may not do. They ended up dead, and that's all that he was worried about."[99]

Despite the blasé and unprofessional attitude of Huntsville officials, Louisiana settled on a lethal injection protocol that used the same three-drug process used in Texas and lacked as many of the same procedural details as that state's protocol. It adopted its first protocol without resolving what the drug dosages would be, when to administer stand-by drugs, or who was qualified to inject the lethal drugs. Louisiana did not base its decision to use the three-drug protocol on scientific study or evidence. It simply followed the lead of Oklahoma and Texas.

Similarly, Jeffrey A. Beard, a former secretary of the Pennsylvania Department of Corrections, noted that Pennsylvania, which chose lethal injection as its execution method in 1990, "adopted almost to a T" the Texas protocol.[100] By the end of that year, a total of twenty-three states had passed lethal injection statutes, and every one of them chose the three-drug combination used in Texas and Oklahoma. This was still true when Nebraska became the thirty-ninth state to adopt the method in 2009. From 1982 until the end of 2009, every execution by lethal injection was done in

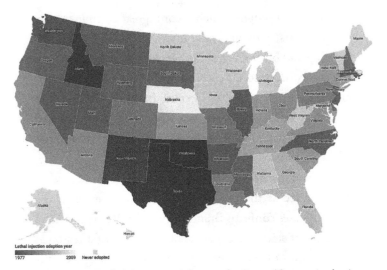

Lethal injection adoption year
1977   2009   Never adopted

FIGURE 8. Lethal Injection Adoption by State. (*Source:* Author)

one way: sodium thiopental to anesthetize the inmate, pancuronium bromide to paralyze them, and potassium chloride to stop their heart.

For scholars who study the diffusion of public policies,
the fact that many states simply copied other states' statutes like this would not be surprising. In the policy
domain, as in other areas of political and social life, imita-
tion is a standard mode of operation.[101] Policy makers in
any one place scan the horizon, looking to other places to
see what works and what doesn't. Policy diffusion generally
occurs in regional configurations and may happen more or
less rapidly.[102] As Oklahoma's and Texas's experiences with
lethal injection suggest, diffusion is often driven as much
by strong personalities as it is by institutional forces.[103]

The federal system, which accords great latitude to state governments, provides the framework within which this learning and borrowing can occur. As Supreme Court Justice Louis Brandeis noted in 1932, the states "are the laboratories of democracy."[104] A state, Brandeis wrote, "may, if its citizens choose, serve as a laboratory; and try novel social and economic experiments without risk to the rest of the country."

The origins of lethal injection and its rapid rise to prominence as the execution method of choice in the United States confirms Brandeis's insight. But it was not a triumph of scientific expertise or the result of a reasoned examination of the advantages and disadvantages of different drugs or drug combinations. And, of course, no real-time testing could be done on the drugs.[105] As law professor Corinna Barrett Lain correctly observes, the origin and diffusion of lethal injection reveals that "across the country, state DOC officials carelessly copied a protocol that had been carelessly designed in the first place."[106]

Reflecting on the history of lethal injection during a 2014 interview, Chapman admitted that when he proposed the three-drug protocol:

> I had absolutely no concept at the time. I was very young. I was not educated in the ways of legislators. I had no idea there was the communication between the states that exist in different areas. This business of lethal injection was a pure sidelight, and the only reason I got involved was at the request of the legislator who was interested in a more humane method of execution, and this is what I suggested. And at the

time when I suggested it, I had no idea, not in my wildest flight of fancy would I have ever thought that it would've mushroomed into what it did.[107]

Lethal injection's origin story is wrapped up in the illusory search for a humane way to execute. This execution method was brought to life by people who might have had good intentions but really did not know what they were doing. Their initial hunches, carelessness, and mistakes laid the shaky foundation on which capital punishment's last half-century would be built.

3 THE COLLAPSE OF THE ORIGINAL PARADIGM

The three-drug combination that A. Jay Chapman first proposed in Oklahoma in the mid-1970s would remain the standard drug protocol for lethal injection in the United States for more than forty years. During those forty years, the meaning of "lethal injection" remained clear and consistent: it referred to those three drugs, to be employed in a similar way across states. In 2009, however, the company that produced sodium thiopental said it would temporarily stop manufacturing the drug, thus depriving states of one of the three drugs in the original protocol. Suddenly, for the first time since lethal injection began to be used, states were forced to develop new drug protocols to carry out their executions. As this chapter describes, those changes led to the unraveling of the original lethal injection paradigm and the three-drug cocktail. But it also came with a number of unexpected consequences that raise serious questions about the viability of lethal injection for state executions.

By 2012, no state in the country still used Chapman's original three-drug formula. Instead, states were executing people with a variety of novel drug combinations. The Supreme Court's decision in *Baze v. Rees* had provided states with wide latitude to experiment with different drugs for their executions.[1] With Chapman's original drug protocol no longer available, execution procedures were moving rapidly into unknown territory.[2]

Baze v. Rees began in 2004 when two death row inmates in Kentucky launched appeals to overturn their death sentences. In their suit, they contended that lethal injection violated the Eighth Amendment because an improper administration of the traditional three-drug protocol could cause "excruciating pain." One of the petitioners, Ralph Baze, had been sentenced to death in Kentucky for the murder of a sheriff, Steve Bennett, and a deputy sheriff, Arthur Briscoe, as they attempted to serve an arrest warrant on him. The second petitioner was Thomas Bowling, who, like Baze, was also on death row for murder. Together, they filed lawsuits challenging the constitutionality of their upcoming executions. They argued that because other execution methods posed a "lower risk of causing pain or suffering," the lethal injection protocol could inflict "unnecessary and wanton... pain." Baze and Bowling proposed two alternative protocols in their suit. The first used only an overdose of sodium thiopental, eschewing the second and third drugs. The second alternative omitted the paralytic agent from the standard protocol while maintaining the first and third drugs.

After the Kentucky Supreme Court upheld the use of lethal injection, Baze and Bowling appealed to the Supreme Court. The court ruled 7-2 against the two men. The plurality opinion, written by Chief Justice John Roberts and joined by Justices Samuel Alito and Anthony Kennedy, found lethal injection to be a constitutional method of execution. Furthermore, the opinion introduced the requirement that any plaintiff mounting an Eighth Amendment challenge to an execution method had to present a "feasible, readily implemented" alternative that would "significantly reduce a substantial risk of severe pain."[3] The court also held that pancuronium bromide, the paralytic in the three-drug combination, served the valid purposes of "hastening death" and "preserving the dignity of the procedure, especially where convulsions or seizures could be misperceived as signs of consciousness or distress."[4]

The *Baze* decision also had important implications for the oversight of the selection of drugs for lethal injection. The court's ruling indicated that it would defer to state choices concerning execution protocols. It assigned the burden of proving that protocols created an unconstitutional risk to plaintiffs rather than requiring states to prove that they did not do so.[5] As a result, states were left with considerable latitude to experiment with new protocols or to stick with the traditional three-drug cocktail. Corrections officials were left to their own devices to decide on execution drugs. However, this did not lead to a rush of new research on how best to develop drug protocols. Instead, many states simply copied each other's

protocols—repeating and codifying drug choices and protocol decisions that were often made without any serious
study of those drugs, and with no more scientific backing
or thoughtfulness than Chapman had used during his
original choice of lethal injection drugs.

In addition to the Supreme Court's ruling in *Baze*,
there was also a specific state-level decision that helped
kick off this lethal injection free-for-all and new period
of experimentation. In 2009, five years after the *Baze*
decision, an Ohio court decided that the state could no
longer use a three-drug execution protocol because doing
so contravened state law.[6] The decision came after a
botched execution when prison officials spent more than
two hours trying to insert needles into the body of an
obviously suffering prisoner, eventually abandoning the
effort. As a result of this failure and the court decision,
Ohio implemented a new drug protocol: a single large
dose of sodium thiopental.[7]

Ohio's decision to stop using the traditional three-drug
protocol was the first step in the decomposition of lethal
injection's original paradigm in the United States. As had
been the case with Chapman's three-drug protocol, other
states quickly followed Ohio's lead, adopting the same one-
drug method because of its relative simplicity.[8] In addition,
some death penalty supporters contend that such one-drug
executions would create far less risk of pain than what
Chapman devised since they would not include drugs, like
potassium chloride, which could cause intense suffering.[9]
Recapitulating the arguments of lethal injection's early

supporters, they said that using an overdose of a barbiturate anesthetic would simply put the condemned inmate to sleep. Whatever their reason, by the end of 2013, thirteen states had switched to such a method.

But just as other states began to adopt Ohio's one-drug execution method, that drug's manufacturer, Hospira— this country's "leading producer of injectable drugs"— temporarily ceased producing sodium thiopental due to a supply chain shortage.[10] At the same time, bowing to pressure from death penalty abolitionist groups, other manufacturers in the United States also decided to limit the distribution of drugs used for lethal injections.[11] Initially, in an effort to keep executions going during this drug shortage, states began to swap drugs with each other. California gave some of its pancuronium bromide inventory to Arizona in exchange for a supply of sodium thiopental. In the eastern United States, Georgia and Arkansas turned to Tennessee for help.[12]

Oklahoma, however, circumvented the sodium thiopental shortages by simply replacing that drug with another. In December 2010, Oklahoma executed John Duty with pentobarbital, a different short-acting barbiturate that had never before been used in an execution.[13] For its second drug, Oklahoma administered vecuronium bromide, a common substitute for the original pancuronium bromide.[14] Finally, potassium chloride was still used as the last drug.

Soon after Oklahoma's first use of pentobarbital, Hospira informed its customers—including death penalty states—

that it would permanently end its sodium thiopental pro-
duction. In a press release announcing its decision, the
company said one reason it was doing so was because it
could not prevent states from using its products in executions.[15] The pentobarbital experiment in Oklahoma showed
other death penalty states that they had an alternative to
sodium thiopental. Nonetheless, because they were used to
sodium thiopental, several states continued to seek that
drug from other manufacturers.

With supply chains in the United States cut off, death
penalty states turned to European drug companies.[16] But
drug companies in Europe and elsewhere were not happy
about corrections departments using their sodium thiopental in executions.[17] Activists were also displeased: the
British anti-death-penalty group Reprieve launched its
Stop the Lethal Injection Project, and manufacturers that
had been selling drugs for executions found themselves
on the receiving end of a shaming campaign.[18] All of
these efforts had the effect of dramatically limiting the
availability of lethal drugs from major drug companies.

But, as law professor Eric Berger has shown, what he
calls the lethal injection "stalemate" did not result solely
from the activity of such anti-death-penalty activists. It
also involved the independent and uncoordinated decisions and work of many different individuals and groups.[19]
They included medical associations, doctors, capital lawyers, federal drug regulators, foreign governments, and
academics. Not all of them were opposed to the death penalty. Each was driven by its own distinctive norms and

motivations.[20] At the same time that the United States Supreme Court was deferring to states and giving them great discretion in how they carried out executions, those individuals and groups made it hard for them to do so.[21] Together, they managed to severely impede or stop the supply of the drugs used in the traditional three-drug cocktail.

As a result, some states turned to alternative drug sources—at one point during this time, Georgia and Arizona purchased 150 vials of sodium thiopental, 450 vials of pancuronium bromide, and 180 vials of potassium chloride from a tiny, obscure drug company called Dream Pharma whose offices were located in the back of a West London driving school.[22] This effort by Georgia and Arizona to purchase lethal drugs from an underregulated distributor overseas points to the lengths to which death penalty states would go to obtain drugs for executions—whether or not they could be confident in those drugs' efficacy—and underscores the lack of meaningful state-level oversight for lethal injection in the United States.

After Georgia and Arizona made this purchase, Reprieve filed suit to block Dream Pharma's continued export of lethal drugs to the United States, and Britain—a country where the death penalty has long been outlawed—imposed an emergency export ban on sodium thiopental in April 2011.[23] Around the same time, worried about an unregulated market for these drugs, a federal district court in the United States required the Food and Drug Administration to enforce its own existing import regulations on execution drugs, further impairing states' ability to obtain sodium thiopental from other countries.[24]

Increasingly unable to replenish their supply of sodium thiopental, several states soon followed Oklahoma's lead and started using drugs like pentobarbital, which did not yet face stringent regulations. Thirteen states held pentobarbital executions in 2011 alone.[25] Some used a three-drug pentobarbital protocol, others used a one-drug pentobarbital protocol. By 2013, the concurrent shifts from three drugs to one drug and from sodium thiopental to pentobarbital combined to produce four distinct lethal injection protocols.[26]

However, the switch to pentobarbital did not alleviate supply pressures.[27] At first, using pentobarbital to replace sodium thiopental appeared to states as a potential solution

TABLE I

Drug Protocols Used Between 2010 and 2013

	One-drug protocol	Three-drug protocol
Sodium thiopental	Ohio, Washington	Texas, Louisiana, Oklahoma, Florida, Mississippi, Virginia, Alabama, Georgia, Arizona
Pentobarbital	Ohio, Arizona, Idaho, Texas, South Dakota, Georgia, Missouri	Oklahoma, Texas, South Carolina, Mississippi, Alabama, Arizona, Georgia, Delaware, Virginia, Florida, Idaho

Drug protocols used in executions from January 2010 through September 2013, by state. In September 2013, states began to adopt even newer drug protocols that eschewed barbiturates, the class of drugs that contains both sodium thiopental and pentobarbital. States that held executions with more than one protocol are listed twice. (*Source:* Author) for their drug shortages. But soon, they found themselves facing the same supply shortages and pushback from manufacturers that they'd faced with sodium thiopental. Soon after Oklahoma began using pentobarbital, the drug's only major producer, a Danish company called Lundbeck, blocked its sale to death penalty states.[28] This problem emerged for other states which sought new drugs for their execution protocols.

For example, as soon as Missouri announced that it would switch to another drug, propofol, that drug's main United States supplier imposed new restrictions on its distribution. The company reached out to health-care providers and warned them that propofol imports could cease entirely if Missouri went ahead with its plan. Faced with "an outcry from the state's anesthesiologists," Missouri's governor ordered corrections officials to halt plans to use the drug.[29] Companies that manufactured other potential lethal injection drugs followed suit when states tried to switch to their drugs.

Increasingly desperate to find ways to obtain drugs necessary for their executions, but unable to secure them from large pharmaceutical companies, some states tried to procure drugs through illegal channels. In one reported purchase, Texas corrections officials hid the fact they were the buyer by using an employee's name and credit card to order a supply of lethal drugs, presumably to conceal their intended use from the pharmaceutical company.[30] The unwillingness of companies to readily provide their drugs for lethal injection also led to price increases and questionable delivery methods. In 2020, for example, Arizona officials spent an astonishing $1.5 million to procure lethal drugs from a source that the state refused to disclose.[31] The Death Penalty Information Center attributes the exorbitant price to the state's need to persuade the distributor to supply the drugs for a non-medical purpose. The vials were shipped to an undisclosed location "in unmarked jars and boxes."

In their efforts to maintain executions in the face of this broader public and private revolt against the practice, death penalty states including Georgia, Texas, Oklahoma, Virginia, Missouri, and South Dakota turned to less regulated means to obtain drugs for their execution protocols. One example of this was their growing reliance on compounding pharmacies to produce small batches of drugs especially for them.[32] Compounding pharmacies first came into existence in the United States in the 1880s. Since the advent of big pharmaceutical companies in the twentieth century, they have taken on the role of producing medications for patients on a case-by-case basis when commercial drugs are unavailable or unusable due to allergies.[33] Unlike larger operations, compounding pharmacies are not subject to extensive regulation by the Food and Drug Administration. Though pharmacists are required to be licensed, licensure requirements vary from state to state, and the laws governing compounding facilities are often lax.

This lack of meaningful oversight has had predictable and sometimes tragic results, including distribution of contaminated drugs, patient deaths, and even jail sentences for compounding pharmacy employees. In 2012, fungal contamination at New England Compounding Center (NECC), a Massachusetts pharmacy, led to a meningitis outbreak that killed more than 100 people and made more than 700 sick.[34] Compounding pharmacies are supposed to produce drugs in sterile conditions, but flies and mold infested NECC's clean room. The pharmacy regularly fabricated prescriptions, used expired ingredients, and shipped drugs before ensuring they were sterile.[35] Though some states and the federal government have since tightened regulations on compounding pharmacies, they are still subject to less oversight than other drug manufacturers.[36]

Despite these problems, states continued to rely on compounding pharmacies to supply drugs for their lethal injections. In October of 2012, South Dakota became one of the first states to use compounded drugs when it executed Eric Robert. Robert was sentenced for beating a prison guard, Ronald "RJ" Johnson, to death while trying to escape the South Dakota State Penitentiary in 2011. At the time of his escape, he was serving eighty years for impersonating a police officer and kidnapping an eighteen-year-old woman.[37] After the injection of pentobarbital, the only drug used in South Dakota's protocol at the time, a media witness reported that Robert cleared his throat, gasped heavily, and then snored for about thirty seconds,[38] keeping his eyes open throughout.[39] Twenty-two minutes later, when the coroner declared Robert dead, he had turned purple. According to Reprieve, an analysis of the compounded pentobarbital used in Robert's execution showed that it was contaminated with fungus.[40]

Texas began to use compounded drugs soon after South Dakota, and, like South Dakota, encountered problems both obtaining and employing them. In 2013, with its supply of pentobarbital—the only drug the state could use at the time—set to expire, Texas initially tried to obtain a new supply from Pharmacy Innovations, a Jamestown, New York compounding pharmacy.[41] This led to a debacle, however. Throughout that year, Texas's Department of Criminal Justice (TDCJ) had been purchasing from Pharmacy Innovations vials of two other drugs—midazolam and hydromorphone—that were not part of the state's lethal injection protocol at the time.[42] Once the pharmacy learned how its pentobarbital would be used, however, the company canceled the order. In order to continue its executions, Texas was forced to turn to other states for help, and Virginia and South Carolina agreed to supply TDCJ with a few vials of manufactured (not compounded) pentobarbital,[43] which Texas then used in September 2013 for the executions of Robert Garza and Arturo Diaz.

Even with the stopgap help from Virginia and South Carolina, Texas still faced a shortage of pentobarbital, and by the end of September, its last properly manufactured drugs had expired. Still, the state pushed forward with its plans to execute Michael Yowell in October for the murder of his parents, John and Carol Yowell, and grandmother, Viola Davis.[44] Unable to purchase pentobarbital from any major drug companies, but needing a drug for Yowell's execution, the state purchased eight vials of compounded pentobarbital from Woodlands Compounding

Pharmacy in The Woodlands, Texas, for $2,800. Concealing its planned use for the drug, Texas placed the order in the name of its Huntsville prison's hospital. Two days later, however, the pharmacy learned what Texas intended to use the drug for, and they asked for the vials back. But TDCJ refused.[45]

On October 9, 2013, Texas executed Yowell with the compounded pentobarbital. Similar to what happened when South Dakota used compounded pentobarbital, Yowell's execution lasted an excruciating twenty minutes. After the injection, Yowell appeared to "struggle for breath several times" before beginning to snore and eventually dying.[46]

The shift toward using less regulated compounding pharmacies for lethal injection drugs continued in the following years. In 2018, ten states sourced their drugs from compounding pharmacies.[47] On occasion, they were forced to stop executions because the drugs the compounding pharmacies had provided seemed contaminated.[48] Because of the many problems that emerged, there have been several legal challenges to the use of compounding pharmacies for lethal injection drugs and much scrutiny. Inmates have filed lawsuits claiming a right to know the source of execution drugs—lawsuits that have delayed and stayed executions.[49] In addition, compounding pharmacies have been the target of protests and lawsuits because of their role in lethal injections.[50]

As a result, states have enacted secrecy statutes aimed at protecting their drug sources. However, these statutes have not always achieved that result. In March 2015, a

Mississippi judge ordered the Department of Corrections to release the names of the compounding pharmacy that supplied the state with pentobarbital. "More than ever," the judge wrote, "the origin, integrity, and composition of lethal injection drugs is a matter of serious public concern." The judge specifically cited "the visible torture of several condemned prisoners in other states last year in botched executions."[51] When pressured, pharmacies have quit the execution drug business or asked for their drugs back, and in 2015, the Alliance for Pharmacy Compounding[52] and the American Pharmacists Association both urged their members to stop compounding execution drugs.[53]

In addition to states' turning to compounding pharmacies for drugs that they can no longer purchase from more regulated manufacturers, other states experimented with novel drugs. In 2013, Florida geared up to conduct the nation's first execution using midazolam hydrochloride[54] as the initial drug in its three-drug protocol.[55] Richard Dieter, executive director of the Death Penalty Information Center called it "an experiment on a living human being."[56] A lethal injection drug expert at the Death Penalty Clinic at the University of California, Berkeley told National Public Radio in 2013, "If [midazolam] does not in fact deeply anesthetize the prisoner, then he or she could be conscious and aware of being both paralyzed and able to experience pain and the experience of cardiac arrest."[57] Nevertheless, Florida's execution proceeded as planned. In 2014, Oklahoma, Arizona, and Ohio also conducted executions with midazolam.

Two of those states, Ohio and Arizona, did not just replace the first drug in the traditional three-drug protocol with midazolam. They also dropped the second and third drugs for hydromorphone, an opiate made from morphine.[58] In both states, the first executions using the new drug combination were botched.

In January 2014, Ohio executed Dennis McGuire using this combination of midazolam and hydromorphone. McGuire had been convicted of raping and murdering a twenty-two-year old pregnant woman, Joy Stewart, in 1989. Witnesses at his execution reported that McGuire made choking sounds and several loud snorts and gasps. He convulsed for roughly ten minutes, his eyes rolling to the back of his head.[59] He tried to sit up, yelling, "I love you. I love you."[60] The execution lasted twenty-four minutes.

Six months later, using the same drug combination that Ohio employed in McGuire's execution, Arizona executed Joseph Wood. Wood was convicted of murdering his girlfriend, Debra Dietz, and her father, Eugene Dietz, in 1989. As discussed later in chapter 5, Wood gasped for air for over an hour before his lawyers filed an emergency appeal with the Supreme Court to halt the prolonged execution. The appeal was denied, and Wood died 117 minutes after his execution began.[61] Since then, the protocol used to kill him has not been used in any execution.

Even as mishaps accumulated, death penalty states continued to experiment with different drugs and drug combinations. Their forays beyond the well-trodden ground

FIGURE 9. Dennis McGuire. (*Source:* AP.)

of barbiturates—the class of drugs to which sodium thiopental and pentobarbital belong—did not end with midazolam. In 2017, when drug manufacturers refused to
provide Florida with barbiturates, the state chose to use a
different sedative, etomidate, in its place. Etomidate is an
ultrashort-acting sedative and anesthetic that has no anal-
gesic (pain-blocking) abilities, and it had never before
been used in an execution.[62]

Florida conducted seven executions with etomidate in
combination with rocuronium bromide and potassium
acetate between 2017 and 2019. That protocol's third drug

was also a novel choice: although Oklahoma inadvertently used potassium acetate instead of potassium chloride in a 2015 execution,[63] no state intentionally used it until Florida made it part of its official lethal injection protocol in 2017. Since adopting this protocol, Florida has used etomidate, rocuronium bromide, and potassium acetate in all of its lethal injections.[64]

Like Florida, Nebraska had trouble acquiring its lethal injection drugs in the latter part of the last decade. After failing for years to find drugs, the state allowed the corrections director to develop a new protocol. In 2018, Nebraska held the only execution conducted in the United States with a four-drug combination when it used diazepam, fentanyl, cisatracurium besylate, and potassium chloride to execute Carey Dean Moore.[65] The first three drugs in the combination had never before been used in an execution.

Moore, who spent thirty-eight years on death row, was convicted of killing two Omaha cab drivers, Reuel Van Ness, Jr. and Maynard Hegeland, in 1979. His was the first execution in Nebraska since 1997 and the state's first lethal injection. Witnesses could not see the entirety of Moore's reaction to the lethal injection because, after the last drug was administered, the curtain in the execution chamber was closed (as allowed in the state's protocol).[66] From the portions of the execution they could see, witnesses said Moore's face turned reddish, then purple, and at one point his abdomen heaved as his breathing quickened. The execution lasted approximately twenty-three minutes.

By the end of 2020, states had used at least ten distinct drug protocols in their executions.[67] To better understand states' changing protocols over time, in Table 2 and Figure 10, we sort them into three different categories: barbiturate combinations, barbiturate overdoses, and sedative combinations.

TABLE 2

Classification of Lethal Injection Drug Protocols.

Classification	Characteristics	Examples
Barbiturate combination	Sodium thiopental or pentobarbital in combination with a paralytic and a heart-stopper	Sodium thiopental, pancuronium bromide, and potassium chloride *(traditional three-drug protocol)* Pentobarbital, rocuronium bromide, and potassium chloride
Barbiturate overdose	Sodium thiopental or pentobarbital on their own	Sodium thiopental alone Pentobarbital alone
Sedative combination	Midazolam, etomidate, or diazepam in combination with other drugs	Midazolam and hydromorphone Etomidate, vecuronium bromide, and potassium acetate

(*Source:* Author)

Some of those protocols were used multiple times, while some were used just once. Even so, the traditional three-drug protocol was all but forgotten. After a decade of experimentation, all that remains of the original lethal injection paradigm is a needle in the inmate's arm and a declaration of death.

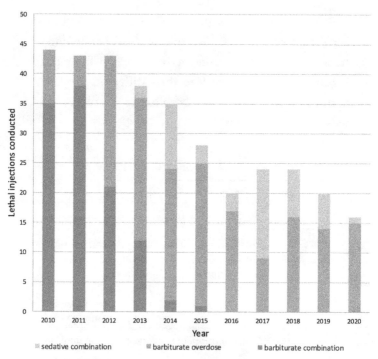

FIGURE 10. Drugs and Drug Combinations by Year of Use.
(*Source:* Author)

4   A DECADE OF MISHAPS

Between 2010 and 2020, the United States carried out a total of 335 lethal injections. The use of this method made up the overwhelming majority of executions (which include those carried out at the state and federal level) during that ten-year period.[1] This high number, along with lethal injection's predominance as the method of choice, demonstrates the remarkable faith the United States had come to place in lethal injection as a humane means of execution. However, as the executions of Jack Jones, Kenneth Williams, and others discussed in previous chapters demonstrate, many problems emerged involving the preparation to put someone to death, the lack of predictability of the drugs themselves or the way they were administered. This chapter looks closely at the growing prevalence of these mishaps. It shows that, despite the efforts of many states to render their problems less visible to public scrutiny, there is increasing evidence that lethal injection is as likely to go wrong as right.

Problems in executions are, of course, nothing new. For as long as this country has used capital punishment, states have encountered problems. Historical data on executions carried out in the United States indicate that from 1890 to 2010, 3 percent were botched in some way.[2] Hangings sometimes resulted in gruesome beheadings and slow asphyxiations. During electrocutions, inmates convulsed and occasionally burst into flames. Lethal gas, billed as yet another humane execution technology, caused its victims to cough, jerk, and writhe in pain for several minutes before death. Lethal injection, as we have already noted, is no exception to this pattern of problems.

After 2009, as the last chapter explained, states were forced to develop new protocols for their lethal injections. This led states to pursue inconsistent and untested approaches to lethal injection, with unpredictable results. To fully capture the nature and extent of the problems that have emerged with lethal injection over the last decade, we examined every execution that took place during this time period. The results of this analysis, which we describe in this chapter, reveal consistent evidence of mishaps before and during the execution: discrete, identifiable moments in an execution when lethal injection faltered.

Some mishaps arose from procedural errors committed by the execution team that showed carelessness for the rights of the condemned. For example, officials sometimes started the injection early, before the inmate could finish their last words. In other cases, these mishaps caused physical pain, such as when executioners had trouble setting intravenous lines or set them incorrectly. Mishaps also included instances of unforeseen bodily reactions to lethal drugs, such as inmates crying out, claiming that the injections burn, coughing, gasping, or heaving their chests. These reactions signal that an inmate underwent unnecessary emotional or physical suffering, or otherwise responded to the execution in a troubling way.

If death by lethal injection was originally conceived as like falling asleep, mishaps signal the ways the method fails to deliver on that promise. And the last decade's lethal injections were rife with such mishaps.[3] For example, in twenty-seven of the lethal injections carried out during that period, or 8.1 percent, executioners struggled to set adequate IVs. One of the most notable examples of this was the infamous 2014 execution of Clayton Lockett.[4]

In 1999, when he was twenty-three, Lockett beat and raped a group of young women before shooting and killing one of them, nineteen-year-old Stephanie Neiman.[5] At his trial, Lockett's counsel offered no defense. After three hours of deliberation, the jury found him guilty of "conspiracy, first-degree burglary, three counts of assault with a dangerous weapon, three counts of forcible oral sodomy, four counts of first-degree rape, four counts of kidnapping and two counts of robbery by force and fear."[6] He "was sentenced to death for first-degree murder, and more than 2,285 years in prison for his other convictions."[7]

FIGURE 11. Clayton Lockett. (*Source:* AP.)

Fifteen years later, after he attempted suicide on the morning of his execution, guards dragged Lockett into Oklahoma's death chamber.[8] Once there, and after having been strapped to a gurney, a paramedic tried several times to place an intravenous line in his arms and feet, but failed to find an adequate vein. After three placement attempts, the paramedic asked a doctor on hand—who was ostensibly there only to check for consciousness and pronounce the time of death—to assist her. Anita Trammell, the warden at the time, "knew [Lockett] was in pain" after being stuck with the needle more than a dozen times. She felt "a sliver of pride" because of how "he was taking it like a man."[9] Fifty-one minutes after starting to place the IV, the paramedic and doctor successfully secured one in Lockett's groin using a painful and invasive cut-down procedure.[10] They covered the IV with a sheet to hide his groin from the witnesses.

At 6:23 p.m., the executioners initiated the flow of midazolam. Lockett looked confused for several minutes as he waited for the drugs to take effect, then closed his eyes. During the first consciousness check, the doctor found that Lockett was still conscious, prompting a two-minute pause before a second check. The second time, the doctor determined that he was unconscious. At this point, the executioners injected the paralytic, vecuronium bromide.

After the paralytic's injection, Lockett moved his feet and head while mumbling, "Oh, man." He began to writhe and struggle against the restraints holding him down. The electric heart monitor showed that his heart rate fell by two-thirds. The doctor again entered the execution chamber and lifted the sheet, revealing a "protrusion the size of a tennis ball" where the IV had failed.[11] Instead of sending the drugs into his bloodstream, they had gone into the flesh of his groin. The warden closed the curtain separating the witness room from the death chamber as the doctor and paramedic scrambled to finish the execution. At 6:56 p.m., the director of the Oklahoma Department of Corrections, who had watched from the witness room, stopped the execution. Ten minutes later, and more than forty minutes after the lethal injection drugs began to flow, Clayton Lockett died. Initial reports said that he died from a heart attack, but an independent autopsy concluded that the cause of death was "judicial execution by lethal injection."[12]

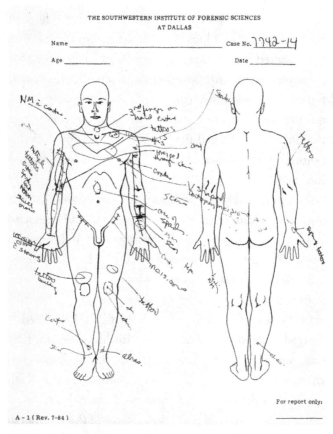

FIGURE 12. Autopsy Diagram of Clayton Lockett. (*Source:* WikiMedia.)

Lockett's botched lethal injection captivated the public in the United States. The *Atlantic* dedicated an 8,000-word cover story to the horrific execution.[13] His Wikipedia page has received more than half a million views and is still edited dozens of times per year as this book goes to press.[14] Few lethal injections go so spectacularly awry and receive this level of media attention. But the risk of mishaps is always present, in part, because of the way lethal injections are carried out, with the people responsible for administering the drugs working from a room separated from the inmate they are charged with anesthetizing and killing. As one medical expert noted, "One would never induce general anesthesia from a remote location. That would be completely, deeply beneath any reasonable standard of care."[15] And if that were not bad enough, lethal injection executions have even taken place in the dark, with the execution team working by flashlight.[16]

Compounding those difficulties is what one reporter correctly labels "the incompetence of the people charged with administering the deadly drugs."[17] Even Dr. Chapman himself has recognized this problem. As he admitted in a 2007 *New York Times* story, "It never occurred to me when we set this up that we'd have complete idiots administering the drugs."[18]

When the execution team manages to set effective lines, or realizes that they cannot do so and stops the execution, the lethal injection process can be undeniably painful. As executioners poke and prod inmates with needles, they fall back on a variety of techniques that inflict substantially more pain than simply placing an IV into an arm. This kind of mishap occurred, for instance, in the attempted execution of sixty-nine-year-old Alva Campbell.

Campbell had been sentenced to death for killing a teenager, Charles Dials, during a carjacking twenty years prior to his execution. In November 2017, an Ohio medical team used an ultraviolet light to probe both of Alva Campbell's arms for a suitable vein. The team poked Campbell twice with a needle in his right arm, then once in his left. But Campbell had lung cancer, chronic obstructive pulmonary disease, pneumonia, and relied on daily oxygen treatments; none of these veins could support the IV. When they tried his left leg, Campbell threw his head back and cried out in pain. The *Columbus Dispatch* reported that after the prison director called off the execution, "Campbell removed his glasses and appeared to rub tears from his withered face."[19]

Even if the IV is set without causing excessive suffering, the rest of the lethal injection process is not necessarily pain-free. Our research reveals that in 4.8 percent of the last decade's lethal injections, inmates complained of pain or severe discomfort at some point during the execution. Because many lethal injections include paralytic drugs, which prevent the condemned from communicating any pain they experience to those who witness or carry out their executions, this figure is likely an undercount of the pain experienced during lethal injections.

One inmate who was able to communicate his pain was Anthony Shore, who was executed for a series of murders that led him to be known as the "Tourniquet Killer."[20]

On January 18, 2018, with IVs already set, Shore apologized to his victims, saying that "no amount of words or apology could ever undo what I've done... I wish I could undo the past, but it is what it is."[21] Soon after the injection of compounded pentobarbital began, Shore cried, "Oh wee, I can feel that it does burn. Burning!" He then shook on the gurney and struggled to breathe before dying thirteen minutes later, according to a witness's sworn affidavit.

The burning sensation that Shore reported occurs with surprising frequency in lethal injections.[22] In fact, this particular mishap may result from specific changes that states have made to their lethal injection protocols. Over time, they have generally increased the amount of each drug that they inject into inmates. For example, Virginia's 1995 drug protocol called for 120 mEq of potassium chloride as its final drug. By 2011, it had doubled the dose to 240 mEq.[23] Similarly, Oklahoma's execution protocol used 100 mg of midazolam when that state executed Clayton Lockett. Soon after, it increased the amount fivefold.[24] These massive doses push lethal injection far outside of the realm of standard pharmaceutical practice.[25]

In a string of executions in 2018 that used a one-drug injection of a large quantity of compounded pentobarbital, inmates complained of a strong burning sensation as the drugs took effect. The first of these executions occurred in Georgia in May, when the state killed forty-year-old Robert Butts. When Butts was eighteen, he and his codefendant asked their victim, Donovan Parks, for a ride to another destination from a Walmart parking lot. Parks agreed, and en route, they ordered him from the car and shot him, execution-style, in the head. Butts spent the majority of his life on death row. On the execution table, twenty years after the murder and a few minutes after the pentobarbital overdose began to flow into his arm, Butts mumbled, "It burns, man."[26]

Twelve days later, Juan Castillo was ushered into Texas's execution chamber. The crime for which Castillo was convicted was similar to Butts's. In 2003, Castillo allegedly lured Tommy Garcia Jr. to a secluded San Antonio road and fatally shot him. Castillo maintained his innocence until the day he died. As the pentobarbital flowed into his body, he lifted his head off the gurney and swore. He could taste the drug, he said, and it burned.[27]

During the last decade, inmates' complaints from the gurney hardly slowed Texas down. In June 2018, Danny Paul Bible, a sixty-six-year-old inmate accused of four killings and nine rapes, was to be executed for the 1979 rape and murder of Inez Deaton to which he had confessed. Bible's lawyers had argued that the severe tremors accompanying his Parkinson's disease would prevent officials from finding a suitable vein and that instead his wheelchair should be put in front of a firing squad, or alternatively, he should be locked in a chamber of nitrous oxide. Their appeals were dismissed, and as it turned out, officials had little trouble inserting the IV. Bible's mother and siblings looked on from the witness area. As the

pentobarbital entered his veins, he muttered: "Burning...
it hurts."[28]

Christopher Young was next to be executed in Texas.
In July, he was put to death for the fatal shooting of Has-
mukhbhai Patel, a San Antonio convenience store owner.
He twice used an obscenity to describe the burning sensation of the pentobarbital. "I taste it in my throat," he
said.[29] But by the time of Young's execution, his verbal
complaints of pain were nothing out of the ordinary—
they were as much a part of the lethal injection process as
preparing the syringes.

In eighty-three lethal injections, the inmate spoke or
made noise after the injection began—utterances that
ranged from screams, to sobs, to slurred sentences. Eric
Scott Branch, for example, did not go quietly. In 2018,
Florida executed Branch for the brutal rape and murder
of a twenty-one-year-old University of West Florida student, Susan Morris. As the lethal drugs began to flow,
Branch started to squirm. "Murderers! Murderers! Murderers!" he screamed. Branch was expressing his opinion
that state- and non-state-sanctioned violence are indis-
tinguishable; earlier in the execution chamber, he had
turned to officials and said they should not have to kill
him. "I've learned that you're good people," he said, "and
this is not what you should be doing."[30] The Associated
Press asked the Florida Department of Corrections spokes-
woman if Branch's outburst was caused by the drugs, to
which she responded there was no indication that was
the case.

Robert Van Hook made a different kind of noise. In 1985, Van Hook strangled and mutilated David Self in a hate crime related to Self's homosexuality. In 2018, the *Akron Beacon Journal* reported that he said "I'm no good" before reciting a Norse poem and singing unintelligibly "until the first of Ohio's three-drug cocktail took effect."[31]

Some inmates make softer, more private sounds. Texas executed Larry Wooten for the brutal double murder of an elderly couple he committed in 1996. Wooten beat eighty-year-old Grady Alexander and his eighty-six-year-old wife, Bessie in their Paris, Texas, home, stabbed the two, and severed their heads. In October 2010, in Huntsville, Texas, the Associated Press reported, simply, "[Wooten] cried as the drugs were administered."[32]

Commonly, inmates exhibited unsettling breathing patterns. Of the executions we studied, seventy-six included coughing, snorting, and other sudden respirations; ninety included snoring. In forty-six, media witnesses noted that the inmate was "gasping" for breath. In eleven executions, observers remarked on the inmate's coughing; in two of these, they described the inmate as apparently "choking." In eight, the inmate was said to be "snorting"; in five, they were "grunting." Eight times, media witnesses described the inmate's heavy, labored exhales as "blowing."

Michael Samra was sentenced to death by the state of Alabama for the 1997 murder of Randy Duke, Randy's fiancée Dedra Mims Hunt, and her two daughters, six-year-old Chelisa Nicole Hunt and seven-year-old Chelsea Marie Hunt. A witness to the 2019 execution wrote that "[Samra's] chest heaved three times in quick succession." Samra's "breathing appeared significantly labored, with his head slightly jerking with each breath for the next minute."[33] He "stretched both hands and slightly raised his left arm, then curled his fingers and dropped his arm." According to anesthesiologist David Lubarsky, "If a patient moves his fingers or hands, that is a clear indicator that they are not anesthetized."[34]

The same night that Alabama put Samra to death, Tennessee executed Don Johnson for the 1984 killing of his wife Carol. It used midazolam as the first of its lethal injection drugs. After the drugs began to flow, Johnson sang hymns, eventually seeming to lose consciousness. But, according to a report in the *Intercept*, "His breathing appeared labored; different witnesses described it as 'snoring' or 'slurping' or 'gasping.' After a consciousness check—and a signal that the execution could continue—Johnson emitted a sharp 'sort of high-pitched 'ah' noise,' as one reporter put it. Another 'counted 33 of whatever that was—a snoring, or a gurgle or a gasp' before the consciousness check, and 28 afterwards."[35]

In 183 of the last decade's lethal injections, or more than half, the inmate moved after the injection began. Many twitched or jerked; some heaved their chests. One such instance of bodily movement occurred in 2018 when Tennessee put Billy Irick to death. More than thirty years earlier, Irick was found guilty of raping and murdering Paula Dyer, a seven-year-old girl. After officials injected midazolam into his veins, he began to "gulp for an extended period of time," choke, gasp, cough, and snore.[36] A witness said that he moved his stomach, moved his head, and "briefly strain[ed] his forearms against the restraints."[37] Such movements suggest that Irick was conscious while the executioners injected the second and third drugs.

According to a Nashville newspaper named the *Tennessean*, the execution deviated from the state's protocol almost as soon as it started.[38] The paper also remarked that Irick's execution took twenty minutes, which it called "longer than average." Later, news reports quoted a doctor who said that Irick almost certainly felt intense pain during his execution.[39] At Irick's request, the state conducted no autopsy after he died.[40]

Some inmates' movements occurred in short, intense spurts. One instance of such sudden movement occurred during Ohio's execution of Darryl Durr. In January 1988, Durr kidnapped sixteen-year old Angel Vincent from her home, raped her, and strangled her with a dog chain. He hid her body in two orange traffic barrels placed end-to-end in Cleveland Park, to be found three months later when boys playing in the park were surprised by the stench. In 2010, the *Norwalk Reflector* reported: "About two minutes after the thiopental sodium began flowing, Durr raised his head and shoulders off the table—even though he was strapped down—and grimaced for about 10 seconds. His head then fell back and his mouth opened wide as the anesthetic took effect." One of the witnesses to Durr's execution then began to cry out "Oh God." His spiritual adviser exclaimed "Oh Jesus."[41]

Inmates often have intense, bodily reactions to the administration of midazolam. There are many documented cases of this. One example was Jerry Correll. In July 1985, Correll stabbed and killed his five-year-old daughter, his ex-wife, her mother, and her sister in Orlando. The *Tampa Bay Times* described the room in which he was executed in 2015 as a small, white death chamber.[42] About two dozen witnesses watched as Correll lay on a gurney, covered with a white sheet below the neck, his hands covered in bandages and his wrists strapped down. Before the injection began, Correll mouthed "Thank you" to a man wearing a cross in the front row. When the lethal injection, which included midazolam, was administered, his upper body convulsed for about ten seconds.[43] His body was then still, but his eyes fluttered and his mouth fell open. The *Tampa Bay Times* wrote: "Thirty years after [the four murders], Correll himself was dead at 59."[44]

Another example of such bodily reactions to midazolam occurred just after the end of the last decade in late October 2021.[45] At that time, Oklahoma resumed executions after a six-year hiatus when it put John Marion Grant to death. Grant had been sentenced for killing Gay Carter, a cafeteria worker, in 1998 with a homemade shank at Dick Conner Correctional Center where Grant was "serving a 130-year prison sentence for several armed robberies."[46] In a news conference after the execution, Associated Press's Sean Murphy reported that soon after the first drug, midazolam, started to flow, Grant began

FIGURE 13. John Marion Grant. (*Source:* AP.)

convulsing. He did so, by Murphy's count, two dozen times and then vomited, with the vomit covering his face and running down his neck. After members of the execution team entered the execution chamber to wipe his face, Grant continued to have what Murphy called full-body "involuntary convulsions."[47] Grant died soon after the second and third drugs in Oklahoma's protocol—vecuronium bromide, a paralytic, and potassium chloride to stop the heart—were administered.

In addition to the many physical movements that occur during lethal injections, dramatic changes in skin color commonly occurred. We identified them in fifty-three executions. For example, when Mississippi executed Paul Woodward in May 2010 for the rape and murder of twenty-five-year-old Rhonda Crane twenty-four years prior, the

Clarion Ledger reported: "By [the time Woodward was declared dead], his feet, his arms and the top of his head had turned a grayish blue."[48] Similarly, after Nebraska's 2018 execution of Carey Dean Moore (whose execution was that state's first ever via lethal injection and which we discussed in the previous chapter) with a novel cocktail of four drugs, media witnesses reported that his face turned red, then "darker purple" and "mottled."[49]

Some of these reactions may be inevitable consequences of death by lethal injection. It works on a microscopic level inside of the body, concealing its operation from view.[50] In fact, medical professionals disagree about how each of the drugs used in lethal injection actually kills.[51] Further complicating the effort to understand what happens during a lethal injection is the paralytic drug used in many protocols. If administered correctly, it prevents inmates from indicating any pain, even involuntarily, making it difficult for witnesses to determine if the condemned suffer.[52]

However, a 2005 study carried out by a surgeon and anesthesiologists suggests that lethal injection drugs used in the standard three-drug cocktail were often not correctly administered or were not given in dosages that ensured the condemned felt no pain.[53] The authors of the study "collected post-mortem data on blood levels of sodium thiopental in 49 executed inmates. Even when the same execution protocol and the same blood sampling procedure was used, they found that levels varied dramatically—from 8.2 to 370 milligrams per litre. In other inmates, mere trace levels were recorded."[54] They also "examined post-mortem blood levels of anesthetic and believe that prisoners may have been capable of feeling pain in almost 90 percent of cases and may have actually been conscious when they were put to death in over 40 percent of cases."[55]

Even if lethal injection drugs are effective, administered properly, and injected in adequate doses so as to render it impossible for the inmate to display what is happening during a lethal injection, this execution method does not deliver on the hopes of its original proponents that it would allow the condemned to die peacefully, as if falling asleep. In September 2020, a National Public Radio investigation found signs of pulmonary edema—fluid filling the lungs—in 84 percent of the 216 post-lethal injection autopsies it reviewed.[56] Some autopsies reveal that inmates' lungs filled while they continued to breathe, which would cause them to feel as if they were drowning and suffocating.

Out of all 335 lethal injections that took place from 2010 to 2020, fifty-two contained mishaps that suggest those inmates suffered from pulmonary edema. During these executions, inmates gurgled or gasped, two uncommon breathing changes that doctors identified as possible signs of pulmonary edema. Since the paralytics prevent some of these signs from showing themselves to outside observers, our count only includes inmates who suffered pulmonary edema while still able to breathe, which accounts for the discrepancy between our count and National Public Radio's.

One case of this pulmonary edema involved the Virginia execution of Ricky Gray in 2017. In 2006, Gray killed four-year-old Ruby Harvey and her sister, nine-year-old Stella Harvey, in their Woodland Heights home, while his accomplice slayed the girls' parents. They then set the home on fire. A few days later, Gray and his nephew killed twenty-one-year-old Ashley Baskerville, her mother, Mary Tucker, and her step-father, Percyell Tucker, in their South Richmond home.[57] A minute into Gray's execution, after midazolam had been injected, he lifted his head, looked around, and moved his toes and legs. He took several deep breaths and made snoring sounds.[58] An autopsy performed on Gray's body found blood-tinged fluid in Gray's mouth and noted that his upper airways contained a foamy liquid. Dr. Mark Edgar, an associate professor of pathology at Emory University School of Medicine, examined the autopsy report and said that its finding of a frothy liquid in the upper airways was very unusual. It was an indication, he said, of acute pulmonary edema.[59]

Dr. Edgar noted that foamy liquid in the upper airways is only found in the most severe cases of that condition, which can come from acute heart failure or actual drowning. The professor said he could not say for certain why the edema happened in Gray's case, but he was sure that, if Gray had been at all conscious during the course of his execution, he would have suffered unbearable torture. Many inmates have claimed that there is insufficient evidence that midazolam can render a person completely insensate, but in the case of Ricky Gray, and in all midazolam executions, we cannot know for sure if the executed was alert.

The occurrence of pulmonary edema, like the burning sensation connected to high-dosage injections, has played a central part in recent legal challenges to lethal injection. In one Ohio case, expert witnesses for the plaintiffs drew upon autopsy reports from past executions as well as a detailed understanding of how midazolam works inside the body to argue that pulmonary edema satisfied what the court called "the first prong of Glossip," that midazolam is very likely to cause severe pain.[60] The "first prong of Glossip" was a criteria the United States Supreme Court first established in 2015 in the case *Glossip v. Gross*, finding that the use of midazolam as the initial drug in Oklahoma's execution protocol did not create a substantial risk of severe pain, compared to known and available alternatives.[61] The court held that any challenge to a method of execution could only succeed if the plaintiff could identify a reasonable alternative that would present a significantly lower risk of pain.

Though the litigation in the Ohio case only concerned midazolam, the hundreds of executions that we reviewed and National Public Radio's investigation suggest that pulmonary edema is a likely side effect of virtually all lethal injection drug protocols. It remains to be seen if the Supreme Court will reconsider its prior approval of midazolam and its deference to states in light of the new evidence about pulmonary edema. However, until it does, lower courts will continue to apply the *Glossip* doctrine that precludes any relief unless inmates can present a readily available alternative.

Alongside the broad evidence of pulmonary edema during recent lethal injections, a review of statements made by witnesses of executions seems to also indicate that executions have become more gruesome to watch. During the last decade, as states switched drug protocols, an increasing number of witnesses or newspapers said that executions were "botched." Between 2010 and 2020, newspapers and independent witnesses used this term to describe twenty-eight of the lethal injections, or 8.4 percent.[62] This label was used to describe only 3.7 percent of barbiturate combination executions. However, newspapers or witnesses labeled 7.3 percent of barbiturate overdose executions as botched, about twice the rate as barbiturate combinations. In sedative combination executions, the rate skyrocketed to 22.4 percent.

The Death Penalty Information Center defines a botched execution as one in which there was a breakdown in, or departure from, the "protocol" for a particular method of execution. Here, the center defines "protocol" broadly, including the state's written protocol as well as the "norms, expectations, and advertised virtues" of the method of execution. Botched executions are therefore "those involving unanticipated problems or delays that caused, at least arguably, unnecessary agony for the prisoner or that reflect gross incompetence of the executioner."[63] The fact that the rate at which newspapers label lethal injections as "botched" has increased over time is made more remarkable by states' intensifying efforts to hide elements of executions from public view. We discuss this trend toward increased secrecy in the following chapter.

Another important example of the problems that have emerged since 2010 in lethal injections across the United States is the amount of time the new drug cocktails take to cause death. There is a striking difference between the length of time barbiturate combination protocols of the pre-2010 era (protocols which also remained in regular use in the first half of the 2010s) took to work compared to the bevy of new cocktails that have recently come into wider use. For example, between 2010 and 2020, one-drug barbiturate overdose executions—which many states began to employ after 2010—lasted 62 percent longer than barbiturate combination executions, including the traditional three-drug protocol. This difference is made even more remarkable by the fact that some states required a short waiting period during barbiturate combination executions after the first drug has been administered. Despite that brief break, one-drug barbiturate overdose protocols took longer. Sedative combinations—novel drug cocktails that came into use during this past decade—have resulted in executions that lasted twice as long as the barbiturate combinations.[64]

When A. Jay Chapman first proposed the original three-drug combination for use in Oklahoma's trailblazing lethal injection bill in the 1970s, he expected each execution to take less than five minutes. As the distin-

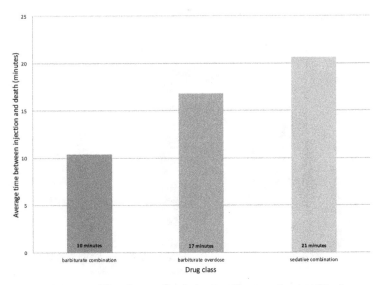

FIGURE 14. How Long after Injection Does an Inmate Live? (*Source:* Author.)

guished sociologist David Garland explains, this expectation was very much in line with the fact that "today's executions put a premium on speed and no-nonsense efficiency."[65] Yet almost none of the lethal injections over the last decade lasted less than five minutes.

Instead, as shown in Figure 15, the average execution time in 2010 was just over nine minutes. In 2020, the average time was over twenty minutes. More than seventy-four of the executions we analyzed took longer than twenty minutes—four times longer than lethal injection's creators expected the method to take. In a few jarring cases, lethal injections took longer than an hour. As we

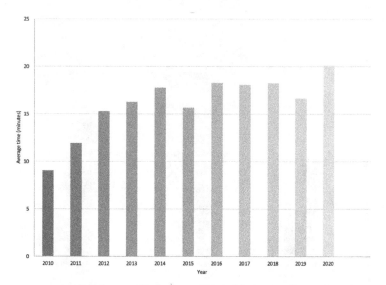

FIGURE 15. Average Duration of Lethal Injection Executions by Year. (*Source:* Author.)

have already noted, Arizona's execution of Joseph Wood in July 2014 execution lasted for two hours.

Such prolonged executions often are the result of state incompetence. They also may be associated with a greater risk that the condemned will experience more suffering during the process. In addition, drawing out the execution process offends the dignity of the inmate, and protecting the dignity of those we execute is central to the Constitution's prohibition of cruel and unusual punishment.

Eight states (Alabama, Arkansas, Florida, Kentucky, Mississippi, Oklahoma, South Carolina, and Tennessee) now permit inmates to decide whether they would prefer electrocution or lethal injection or authorize the former if the latter is unavailable. Inmates choose electrocution because of lethal injection's extended duration. In February 2020, Nicholas Sutton became one of these inmates. Of Sutton's decision, the *New York Times* reported: "'When everything works perfectly, [lethal injection] is about 14 minutes of pain and horror,' said Stephen Kissinger, an assistant federal community defender who has represented Mr. Sutton... 'Then, they look at electrocution, and how long does it take?'"[66]

The answer to that question is that an electrocution could, when it goes off as planned, kill in a little over a minute. Such a rapid electrocution occurred in 2007, when Daryl Holton was pronounced dead in Tennessee after two twenty-second jolts separated by a fifteen-second pause.[67] Although electrocution often acts fast, delivering a quick but violent death, speed is not guaranteed. In 1985, in Indiana, William Vandiver, who murdered and dismembered his father-in-law, Paul Komyatti, Sr., went to the electric chair. Five cycles of current were administered to him over the course of seventeen gruesome minutes.[68] Yet knowing this Nicholas Sutton still chose to die by the chair, showing that there is no method of execution that does not come laden with the risk of a harrowing and torturous death.

States have responded to the kind of problems with lethal injection that prompt such choices by increasing secrecy.[69] In addition, they have refined and adapted their protocols in an effort to make it harder to say when an execution goes awry. Such behavior may not be surprising to anyone who has studied or worked in a complex bureaucracy, but it nonetheless offers further evidence that lethal injection has gone from being this country's supposedly most humane method of execution to being one of its most problematic and embarrassing.

5 STATE RESPONSES

After 2009, when states were struggling to find reliable drug suppliers and experimenting with new drug cocktails to use in executions, there was a simultaneous explosion of media coverage of lethal injection mishaps. In an overview of reporting about botched lethal injections, law professor Jody Madeira observed that "news coverage of flawed lethal injections skyrocketed in 2014 from a yearly average of approximately 100 articles from 2010 to 2013 to approximately 1300 articles per year in 2014."[1] The increased media coverage occurred in step with a steady decline in the percentage of people in favor of the death penalty.[2] These developments applied additional pressure on states to avoid, or hide, mishaps, lest the death penalty fall into further disfavor.

States responded to this growing pressure to avoid mishaps in two ways: First, some departments of corrections modified their execution procedures in an attempt to make mishaps less likely. Such changes included adding consciousness checks, mandating that the IV be clearly visible, and inserting backup lines in case the primary line fails. On the other hand, some states chose to make it harder to identify or label any irregularity in the execution chamber as a departure from their protocols and procedures. They introduced greater ambiguity and discretion into their procedures. Doing so afforded executioners more flexibility to act when something went wrong. Many states also have attempted to keep their procedures and drug suppliers secret from inmates and the public. The responses, specificity and obfuscation, are not mutually exclusive. In fact, as states added some steps to prevent mishaps, they often made other steps less specific.[3]

AVOIDING MISHAPS: PROCEDURAL SPECIFICITY

As the original lethal injection paradigm began to decompose, and the three-drug protocol was replaced by others, death penalty states attempted to avoid preventable error with procedural adjustments. One important example of this is the waiting time a number of states instituted between injections of each drug in the protocol. If the executioners inject the second or third drugs before the first drug anesthetizes the inmate, the condemned will suffer excruciating pain. Similarly, paralytics must have time to immobilize the inmate or their pain will be apparent to witnesses as the condemned jerk and squirm on the table. In an effort to prevent this excruciating pain or bodily reactions, in the late 2000s and early 2010s, nine states began to specify waiting periods between the injection of each drug in the lethal cocktail.[4]

States have used a guess-and-check approach in determining the appropriate duration of these waiting periods. One particularly instructive case is Virginia, which in March 2021 became the first southern state to abolish the death penalty. During the decade before this decision, the state revised its lethal injection protocol several times. In the text of its October 2010 version, the state made no mention of waiting periods. It also required the use of Chapman's three drugs.[5]

By 2012, although Virginia was still using a three-drug protocol, it had stopped requiring Chapman's original version, as the drugs for that original combination were no longer easily obtainable.[6] In this new protocol, the state called for its lethal injections to start with pentobarbital, but also called for a thirty-second waiting period after the first drug's injection. By February 2014, Virginia revised its regulations again. This time they noted the first drug in its three-drug protocol could be any one of three drugs— sodium thiopental, pentobarbital, or midazolam—with that decision left up to the warden's discretion.[7] They also stipulated that, regardless of the drug chosen, the procedure would include a two-minute waiting period after its injection.[8]

Other states' waiting periods differed in duration. This was the case even when those states were using exactly the same combination of drugs or the same type of drug protocol (three-drug or one-drug barbiturate). For example, protocols in Idaho and Delaware (developed in 2011 and 2012 respectively) both called for a waiting period after the injection of pentobarbital and before the next drug. But while Idaho required three minutes, Delaware required only two.[9] Similarly, as states began to allow additional doses of lethal drugs to be injected if the first round did not cause the inmate to die, the waiting periods between these injections have differed. Oklahoma[10] has instructed officials to wait five minutes for the inmate to die; California,[11] Delaware,[12] South Dakota,[13] and Utah[14] have required ten minutes; Kentucky[15] has required twenty.

Some states do not specify the length of this period at all, only directing officials to wait "sufficient time." Ohio's 2016 protocol, like Virginia's in 2014, allows officials to choose the first drug from among sodium thiopental, pentobarbital, and midazolam;[16] Kentucky's 2018 protocol does as well.[17] But while Kentucky found it necessary to ensure that twenty minutes passed before more of the chosen drug is injected, Ohio's procedure leaves the duration completely up to officials in the moment.

Though some of these specific adjustments, like a precisely defined waiting period, may make the lethal injection process appear, on paper, more precise and mechanical, the lack of uniformity across states points to the lack of empirical grounding supporting such specificity. States take a trial-and-error approach to protocol development; they don't really have any idea about the most appropriate period of time to wait for the inmate to become insensate.

Following an execution, the only person officials could ask to definitively determine if the waiting period was effective is dead. Therefore, while the protocols are specific in certain places, they are also arbitrary.

After 2010, when this new period of experimentation began, seven states started to require that officials conduct "consciousness checks" on the condemned inmate.[18] These consciousness checks were instituted as part of an effort to minimize the risk of inmate suffering and also to help the state save face if executions went badly, something that had become more pressing as media scrutiny of lethal injections increased. During these checks, executioners must evaluate an inmate's consciousness with auditory and physical stimuli between the first and second drugs. For example, in its August 2012 protocol, Pennsylvania instructed officials to close the curtain and call the inmate's name in a loud voice before "assess-[ing] consciousness of the inmate by tactile stimulation... touching the inmate's shoulder and brushing the inmate's eyelashes."[19]

As part of this effort to enact urgent safeguards against the risk of mishaps during lethal injection, a few states also added specificity about the placement of IVs, especially after Clayton Lockett's botched execution in 2014. After that execution, Oklahoma added a number of mishap-preventing and mishap-detecting provisions to its lethal injection protocol.[20] It required officials to record the number of IV insertion attempts, read the drug name out loud before its administration, leave the IV in the inmate after death for a medical examiner to see, and ensure the IV insertion remained visible.

One area that shows how little accord there is among death penalty states in how to conduct a lethal injection relates to the actual insertion sites of IVs. In 2005, most death penalty states made no mention of preferred insertion sites. (The federal government and Missouri did specify that an IV might be inserted through the painful femoral vein, which runs from the upper thigh to the pelvic area.[21]) After 2010, eight states began to provide lists of ordered preferences for a large number of insertion sites. [22] But other states did not bother to mention this. Indeed at one or another point during the last decade, protocols from at least thirteen states indicated no preference for an IV site, leaving that decision for the execution team to make.[23] Additionally, four states[24] have, sometime after 2010, explicitly called for a "cutdown" procedure in order to place a central venous line (in the chest) when necessary. Three of them currently call for it. Protocols in four additional states allow a central venous line placement without prohibiting a cutdown.[25] This variation, however, reveals how little understanding states have about how to effectively carry out lethal injections.

In contrast to the lists of possible IV sites in today's protocols, Ohio's 2004 protocol only briefly mentions IV access.[26] It records a preference for setting IVs into the inmate's arms, but does not require that the execution team ensure the IVs are working. In 2009, well before

Lockett's ill-fated execution in Oklahoma, Ohio began to specify that executioners should use a saline drip to test the IVs, perform vein assessments ahead of time, and ensure that the IV insertion points are visible throughout the execution.[27]

Procedural specificity is also found in parts of protocols that identify decisional contingencies (if, then) in the lethal injection process. We call this "branching." From 2010 to 2020, many lethal injection protocols came to resemble decision trees with many branches, rather than a simple set of instructions.

Fourteen states adopted one or more elements of branching, providing additional instructions in case IV lines cannot be established, drugs do not cause unconsciousness or death, or an IV line fails.[28] These instructions, which frequently introduced new complexity into the execution procedure, further illustrate states' efforts to create a reliable protocol for lethal injection executions. For example, Arizona's 2015 protocol included several branches to address issues in the execution chamber, including a situation in which the execution team cannot establish a second site, or even any sites at all. It reads:

> In the event that a patent intravenous infusion site cannot be established, the IV Team shall be directed by the Deputy Director, or designee, to evaluate other possible infusion sites. All effort will be made to establish two (2) unrelated intravenous infusion sites. *If one (1) patent infusion site is established, and a second site proves to be a futile effort,* the Deputy Director, or designee, may direct the IV Team to

suspend further action to establish a second site and proceed with one site. *In the case that no patent infusion site is established after reasonable attempts as determined by the IV Team,* the Deputy Director, or designee, will direct the IV Team to suspend further action and thereafter summon trained, educated, and experienced person(s) necessary to establish a primary IV line as a peripheral line or as a central venous line. (emphasis added)[29]

This excerpt addresses a situation in which the IV team cannot establish a second site, explicitly allowing officials to proceed without it. A second site, however, would ensure that if one IV line fails, another is available to complete the execution quickly and without prolonging the inmate's suffering. The Arizona protocol also accounts for a situation in which the execution team cannot establish any sites at all. In that case, additional personnel are required, and the protocol invites them to employ more invasive procedures. In this way, added specificity accounts for more potential contingencies such that officials are never acting outside the purview of the protocol. Rather than constrain officials in order to make executions more efficient and reduce this inmate's suffering, this specificity gives officials explicit permission to take a wider variety of actions.

Three states—Arizona, Idaho, and Oklahoma—include a provision specifying when officials should stop an execution and try to save the inmate's life. They establish contingency procedures to revive the inmate in case they go into cardiac arrest as the lethal injection is prepared. Using language similar to the other two states, Idaho's 2012 protocol reads as follows: "An automated external defibrillator (AED) will be readily available on site in the event that the offender goes into cardiac arrest at any time prior to dispensing the chemicals; trained medical staff shall make every effort to revive the offender should this occur, unless the offender has signed a do not resuscitate (DNR)."[30]

This type of contingency procedure suggests that maintaining state control is central in executions. Though the inmate may be in the execution chamber and destined to die, his death must only be caused by the execution drugs. If events occur that threaten the state's control over the inmate's death, specific measures must be taken to regain it. Further, by acknowledging that an inmate may be under such intense emotional duress that he goes into cardiac arrest while awaiting the injection, the protocol makes a naturally occurring heart attack a foreseen and prepared-for occurrence in the execution chamber—something normal, something expected for which the executioners have a plan.

In this way, protocols provide executioners with specific methods to redress mishaps as they arise. Further, by acknowledging many possibilities, states try to ensure that fewer events fall outside the purview of lethal injection protocols and that problematic lethal injections are difficult to critique. Additionally, states view these increases in specificity as helping to imbue lethal injection with legitimacy after problematic executions. By making procedures more specific, states implicitly signal that lethal injection can be improved with better procedures and that they are committed to such improvement.

In her essay "The Ghosts in the 'Machinery of Death,'" Jody Madeira, who we quoted at the opening of this chapter, suggests that many of the mistakes made during executions have been normalized in the lethal injection paradigm. She describes how the reforms states have instituted, while intended to reduce mistakes, may actually help create environments in which mistakes occur.[31] "Corrections has long explored execution methods through a 'learning-by-doing' process," she writes, "and may interpret each botched execution as a unique event instead of a patterned consequence of haphazard lethal injection reform."[32] By amending their procedures, states treat lethal injection mishaps as anomalies—wrongs that can be righted with procedural tweaks. Mistake has a vital role in this cycle of error, reconciliation, and relegitimization.

OBSCURING MISHAPS IN LETHAL INJECTION: SECRECY, AMBIGUITY, DISCRETION

At the same time as they tried to deal with mishaps by adding specific checks to their procedures, death penalty states have also tried to obscure the identification and perception of mishaps by hiding executions, and information related to executions, from public view. According to the Death Penalty Information Center, of the seventeen states that carried out executions between 2011 and 2018, fourteen prevented witnesses from seeing at least one part of the execution, fifteen prevented witnesses from hearing the sounds of the execution, and sixteen concealed the source of the drugs used.[33] All seventeen prevented witnesses from finding out the time when lethal drugs were administered.[34]

The results of these restrictions are more or less what the states have hoped for: as states hide more of their procedures and executions, it becomes increasingly difficult to say that, or when, an execution went wrong. The implications of this lack of transparency are significant. As law professor Corinna Barrett Lain writes: "No transparency means no public scrutiny to trigger outrage over these decision-making processes so that democracy can do its thing. And no record-keeping or other rule-making requirements mean no processes for inmates to challenge, and no records by which courts can determine whether a DOC's decision-making was arbitrary and capricious."[35]

Courts demand that evidence challenging a protocol be highly detailed and specific, so this lack of transparency around what occurs in the execution chamber greatly inhibits inmates' ability to challenge the conduct of their upcoming executions. Courts require inmates to produce evidence of actual errors that occurred under conditions similar to those in which they will be executed. These descriptions must be detailed accounts of an execution gone wrong in that particular state. Additionally, courts have repeatedly noted that they will not consider the "risk of accident" associated with a state's protocol but will consider only the constitutionality of the protocol as written. As Madeira writes: "Though the state executes in the name of 'the people,' it is now increasingly impossible for citizens to learn what their state is doing. This opaqueness is dangerous to inmates and to citizens alike; it is our democratic right and privilege to decide what should be done about current lethal injection quandaries to determine where we want to draw the line, and what measures and outcomes are acceptable."[36]

States prevent witnesses from viewing the entirety of the execution in several ways. One way is by closing the curtain between the execution chamber and the viewing window. In twenty-two executions between 2010 and 2020, the curtain was closed after witnesses had been ushered into the viewing room. In some instances, the curtain closure is regularly scheduled. For example, Ohio's protocol calls for the curtain to be closed as officials assess the inmate's status and declare death. But curtain closures, whether scheduled or unexpected, create gaps of time wherein witnesses cannot see the inmate's reaction to the drugs.

Nebraska's protocol does not call for the curtain to be drawn at particular junctures in a lethal injection, but it does not proscribe curtain closures either. Much of the state's 2018 execution of Carey Dean Moore was hidden from witnesses by a closed curtain. The Associated Press reported that the drugs began to flow into Moore at 10:27 the morning of August 14, 2018. The prison warden closed a curtain over the media's viewing window at 10:39 and did not open it again until about fourteen minutes later. Moore was declared dead at 10:47. The curtain was opened six minutes after that time to reveal Moore's body. It remained open for only forty seconds.[37]

While witnesses did see that Moore gasped as the injection took effect and that his face turned red, then purple, the majority of the process was hidden from view. The Death Penalty Information Center wrote that, after Moore's execution, prison officials acknowledged that this curtain closure "[prevented] the reporters from witnessing Moore's reaction to that drug."[38] Witnesses could not be sure whether other mishaps occurred as Moore died by a never-before-used mixture of four drugs, which were selected by the Department of Corrections director due to shortages of other drugs.

Some legal challenges have been mounted in an effort to increase the visibility of executions. In the wake of Virginia's problematic 2017 execution of Ricky Gray, in which there was an unexplained half-hour delay as his IVs were inserted, Virginia revised its lethal injection protocol to make it less transparent.[39] In late 2019, four Virginia media organizations filed suit in Richmond's federal district court, seeking to compel the Department of Corrections to eliminate scheduled curtain closures that, the suit alleges, have prevented the public from observing crucial details of the execution process.[40] The suit challenged Virginia's 2017 execution protocol, which delays opening the curtains to the witness room until after the IV lines have been established and prevents witnesses from observing officials' preparation of the inmate for execution.

The plaintiffs alleged that the state's protocol hid "critical elements of the execution process, and thus violate the public's qualified First Amendment right to observe an execution in its entirety."[41] The plaintiffs further argued that limitations on what witnesses can see during Virginia executions "severely curtail the public's ability to understand how those executions are administered, or to assess whether a particular execution violates either the Constitution or the state's prescribed execution procedures, or is otherwise botched."[42]

Just as they increasingly occlude from sight events inside the chamber, states try to silence an execution's sounds. In July 2014, as Joseph Wood was lying on the gurney in Arizona's death chamber, he gasped, choked, and struggled to breathe for nearly two hours. According to witnesses "Wood [gasped] more than 600 times over the course of an hour and 40 minutes... One witness likened it to the movements a fish makes when it's taken out of water."[43] Following Wood's botched execution, seven death-row prisoners and the First Amendment Coalition of Arizona filed a lawsuit on the grounds that the First Amendment guaranteed access to the sounds of executions. The ruling in the case barred the state from turning off the microphone in the execution chamber after the IV line is placed. Although granting a right of access to the sounds of the execution, the court ruled that the First Amendment did not encompass the right to information about execution drugs or personnel.

Legal scholars, journalists, and advocates have criticized secrecy statutes. According to death penalty scholar Deborah Denno, they "make it difficult—if not impossible—to evaluate the constitutionality of lethal injection."[44] As a result, the American Bar Association "urg[es] all jurisdictions that impose capital punishment to publish their execution drug protocols 'in an open and transparent manner,' require public review and comment on proposed protocols, and require disclosure of 'all relevant information regarding execution procedures.'"[45] Similarly, the Death Penalty Information Center argues that secrecy statutes are fundamentally at odds with democracy in the United States. The organization asserts that "the growing secrecy that shields current state efforts to carry out executions poses significant challenges to the rule of law and to the legitimacy of the democratic institutions administering capital punishment."[46]

In addition to doing more to hide what goes on in executions, states responded to mishaps by making their protocols *less specific* at certain points during their executions. They introduced greater ambiguity in the language governing crucial parts of their protocols. For example, even as states have added more checks to ensure that IVs are working, they allowed executioners to attempt to set lines for longer periods of time and in more places on the inmates' bodies. They did so by requiring that officials act in a "reasonable" manner without defining what counts as reasonable. Thus, Ohio's procedure, exemplifying the language used in many post-2010 death penalty protocols, allowed its IV team to "make such a number of attempts to establish an IV site as *may be reasonable*" (emphasis added).[47]

States also have added ambiguity concerning the amount of time an execution is supposed to take. No state procedures now specify a maximum time that can pass between injection and death. As a result, lethal injection's critics cannot point to a specific regulation in order to hold states accountable for long and painful executions. In fact, the refusal of courts or legislatures to impose time constraints on executions has been integral to lethal injection's survival. As we noted above, the average length of a lethal injection in 2011 was under ten minutes. By 2012, the average time had increased to fifteen minutes, and by 2020, it was twenty minutes. Yet, recent challenges to lethal injection on the grounds that this increased time frame is unacceptable have all failed.

One example of these efforts is the Tennessee Supreme Court's 2017 case *West v. Schofield*.[48] In that case, several inmates challenged the constitutionality of Tennessee's one-drug pentobarbital protocol, partially on the grounds that it creates a substantial risk of a lingering death. One of their expert witnesses reviewed thirty pentobarbital executions conducted in Georgia, Ohio, and Texas and found that all of them resulted in death within thirty minutes of the first injection. Because no procedural, legal, or judicial standard of "lingering death" had ever been established, the Tennessee court had to decide whether a half-hour death constituted cruel and unusual punishment. Without explicitly affirming a thirty-minute standard for lethal injections, it found the protocol to be constitutional.

In fact, the court held that executions lasting as long as an hour may be permissible: "The Plaintiffs cite to no authority supporting the proposition that an execution requiring up to an hour for death to result is a 'lingering death' prohibited by the Eighth Amendment, particularly when the inmate is unconscious for all but the first few seconds of the process."[49] According to the court, the Supreme Court's holding in *Kemmler* that the Eighth Amendment prohibits lingering death only prohibits a state from killing someone by withholding food or medical care. Lethal injections can go on indefinitely without violating the law.

The fact that inmates have no legal right to a quick execution significantly reduces the burden on states to maximize efficiency and produce rapid deaths. It also makes it easier for prison officials to explain away excruciatingly long executions. Texas executed Barney Fuller in October 2016 for his shooting a couple to death thirteen years earlier. Fuller's execution lasted for thirty-eight minutes. The *Chicago Tribune* mentions the execution's duration only briefly, writing: "The time between when the drug was injected and when [Fuller] was pronounced dead was somewhat longer than normal. 'Each person is unique in how his body shuts down,' prison agency spokesman

Jason Clark said, commenting on the extended time."[50] By the legal standards in place and states' prevailing lethal injection norms, the spokesman owed the public no further explanation.

In December 2014, in the wake of Joseph Wood's execution, CNN ran the headline: "Two hour execution followed correct protocol, says independent report." The article reads: "Staff performance in no way contributed to the extended time lapse from initiation of the drug protocol to pronouncement of death… [T]he execution was not 'botched' in comparison to what occurred in Oklahoma with Clayton Lockett."[51] After even such a gruesome display of state-sanctioned death, the vagueness of the state protocol insulated lethal injection from criticism.

According to Arizona's official report, the officials carrying out Wood's execution did not misstep. They administered fourteen doses of midazolam; the officials deemed this necessary to kill, and doing so fell within the bounds of the protocol. Lethal injection's champions use the protocols, and officials' adherence to them, to demonstrate its effectiveness: officials didn't do anything wrong, and so there is nothing to critique. This protocol-based argument misses a larger point: officials may not do anything that contravenes the governing regulations, and yet things may go terribly wrong.

States try to make it harder to say when mishaps occur by explicitly or implicitly authorizing officials to exercise discretion. Some state protocols set extremely broad expectations about how long the IV insertion is supposed to take. In 2017, Kentucky provided a one-hour window for the IV insertion process before an execution must be stopped.[52] It revised its protocol in 2018 and expanded that window to three hours. Similarly, in 2016 Ohio made its lack of a standard explicit, writing in its protocol that the IV insertion team should take "as much time as necessary."[53]

In 1987, Doyle Hamm was sentenced to death for murdering Patrick Cunningham during a robbery. On February 22, 2018, in Alabama, the sixty-one-year-old was being prepped for lethal execution at the Holman Correctional Facility. Years of drug use, as well as chemotherapy following a diagnosis of lymphoma cancer and carcinoma four years prior to the execution date, left Hamm with severely compromised veins. In the months leading up to his execution, Hamm's attorney, Columbia Law School Professor Bernard Harcourt, had warned that Hamm had no accessible veins and thus a lethal injection attempt would constitute cruel and unusual punishment in his case.[54] The state went forward with the execution nonetheless.

Officials spent two and a half hours searching for a suitable vein, leaving Hamm with a dozen puncture marks, including six in his groin. The attempts damaged his bladder and penetrated his femoral artery. As the night went on, the project of putting Hamm to death became more urgent. His death warrant would expire at midnight, and thus if officials could not kill him before the clock struck twelve, they could not kill him that night at all.

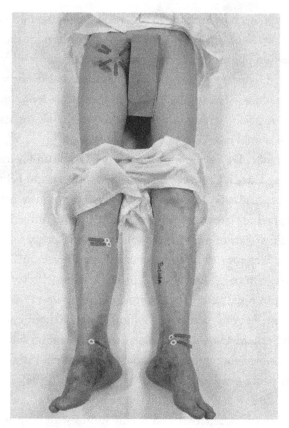

FIGURE 16. Doyle Hamm after execution attempt.
Photo taken at Holman Prison, Atmore, Alabama,
on February 25, 2018. (*Source:* Bernard E. Harcourt.)

Finally, exasperated officials and medical personnel
called off the execution. The time constraint on Hamm's
execution was not imposed by the lethal injection protocol. The death warrant primarily exists to establish a date
for the execution, though it generally sets a time limit of

twenty-four hours. In a sense, this is the only standard constraining the duration of a lethal injection, and, as can be seen in Hamm's case, it does a poor job of it. Hamm joined a grim fraternity of a few inmates whose lethal injection was botched, but who lived to tell about it.[55]

Alabama Prison Commissioner Jeff Dunn told reporters after Hamm's near-death experience that "I wouldn't necessarily characterize what we had tonight as a problem."[56] Yet in the wake of the failed execution attempt, Hamm filed suit in both state and federal courts. A doctor's expert report submitted to the courts read as follows:

> The doctor advanced a needle into Mr. Hamm's groin. Mr. Hamm felt multiple needle insertions, and with each insertion he felt multiple probing advance-withdrawal movements. It is not clear whether local anesthetic was administered. Mr. Hamm felt the needle penetrating deep into his groin and pelvis. Mr. Hamm stated that this probing was extremely painful. Twice during needle advancement he experienced sudden sharp deep retropubic pain. The doctor requested a new needle several times. During this time Mr. Hamm began to hope that the doctor would succeed in obtaining IV access so that Mr. Hamm could "get it over with" because he preferred to die rather than to continue to experience the ongoing severe pain. He was shivering and trembling from a combination of fear and the fact that the room was very cold.[57]

Hamm reached a confidential settlement with the state. As a result of this settlement, Alabama would not try to execute him again. His claim for monetary damages also was dropped. Hamm died from cancer on Alabama's death row on November 28, 2021, a little less than three years after the failed execution.

Protocols also frequently grant discretion when the officially prescribed drug dosage is insufficient to kill. Nineteen states' protocols have allowed officials overseeing the execution to inject additional doses as they see fit.[58] Dosing lethal injection drugs, however, is no straightforward task. John DiCapua, an anesthesiologist at North Shore-LIJ Health System in Great Neck, New York, notes that the kind of drugs states use in lethal injection require different doses in order to be effective in different individuals. Midazolam, for example, requires a fairly variable dose; it may require ten times the dose to achieve unconsciousness in one person versus another, DiCapua said.[59] Some people may also have developed a tolerance to certain drugs, requiring a larger dose to be effective. These types of judgments are best made by a medical professional rather than prison staff. However, as we said elsewhere, it is unlikely that a midazolam dosing mistake would be obvious to an execution's observer, as the paralytic would prevent the inmate from showing signs of pain even if the observer were alert to it. Further, thirteen death penalty states have left the length of the waiting period between rounds of drug injections completely up to prison officials.[60] A waiting period cut short could mean an inmate has not yet been properly anaesthetized and would therefore be conscious as the painful lethal drugs entered his veins.

Occasionally, permission for a second injection is accompanied by permission for a range of other actions. Oklahoma's 2015 protocol allows the execution team to close the curtain, remove all of the witnesses, inject additional doses, and "determine how to proceed"—a generous grant of discretion that gives officials room to change the procedure on the fly without any accountability.[61]

Moreover, fourteen death penalty states no longer specify a particular drug cocktail, as they all had done before 2009.[62] Instead, they allow officials to choose from a menu of drugs and drug combinations. Idaho's 2012 protocol reads, "which option is used is dependent on the availability of chemicals," making it explicit that these menus serve to enable executions to proceed in the face of drug shortages.[63] Similarly, Mississippi's 2015 protocol allows officials to choose between three options for the first drug (sodium thiopental, pentobarbital, and midazolam) and two options for the second drug (pancuronium bromide and vecuronium bromide), meaning officials can mix-and-match lethal drugs in six possible ways.[64]

In 2017, Nebraska's Department of Corrections left both the type and quantity of drugs up to the department director's sole discretion. The protocol reads:

> The Director shall determine which substance or substances and quantity are to be employed in an execution by lethal injection. If more than one substance is to be employed in an execution by lethal injection, the first substance injected must be capable of rendering the convicted person unconscious. The Director's determination of the substance or substances to be employed in an execution by lethal injection may be based on the availability of necessary substances.[65]

Further expanding the prerogative of the director, the protocol states that: "The Director has the authority to create and modify this protocol." This enormous grant of discretion is what enabled a Nebraska prison to experiment on Carey Dean Moore in 2018 with an untested cocktail of four drugs.

It is common for state legislatures to pass the buck for making even the most consequential decisions about lethal injection.[66] They delegate them to correctional departments, which wield immense authority in determining, developing, and enforcing the protocols which describe lethal injections forms and procedures. They exercise that power largely out of public view. From there, correction departments may further delegate responsibility to prison officials or assign it, as in Nebraska, to the department's own director.

Yet, correctional officials are often ill-equipped to make sound decisions about lethal injection's implementation. As Corinna Barrett Lain notes:

> Lethal injection statutes provide no guidance whatsoever to the corrections departments that must implement them. Prison personnel have no expertise in deciding what drugs to use or how to perform the procedure. And the usual administrative law devices that we rely on to bring transparency and accountability to the agency decision-making process are noticeably absent. The culmination of these irregularities is a world where lethal injection drug protocols are decided by Google searches and other decision-making processes that would be patently unacceptable in any other area of administrative law.[67]

As Lain points out, this is an inversion of the notion that death is a unique form of punishment which must be inflicted with the utmost care and attention to detail. She writes: "In the execution context, death penalty exceptionalism means that the minimal standards that ordinarily attend administrative decision-making do not apply. Death is different, but in a perverse way."[68]

Ambiguity and discretion provide executioners with a kind of blank check that brings lingering, fraught deaths into the fold of legally acceptable executions. Ambiguous language allows officials to elide details and avoid the specific provisions that once protected inmates from long or painful executions. The discretion that protocols now afford executioners provides them with the latitude to modify execution procedures on the fly. Executioners can do what they think necessary to kill the inmate while acting within the authority granted by state protocols.

In December 2016, Alabama executed Ronald Smith for the 1994 slaying of a convenience store clerk, Casey Wilson.[69] Smith had challenged Alabama's execution protocol, claiming that midazolam, the first drug in the three-drug protocol that would be administered to him, would sedate him without rendering him insensate to the burning feeling induced by the following two drugs. His challenge failed, and the execution went on.

His execution lasted for thirty-four minutes, and for thirteen minutes after the first drug was injected, Smith struggled for breath, heaved his chest, coughed, and clenched his fist. Even after his second consciousness check, in which officials declared him unconscious, he moved his hands and arm. His left eye appeared to be slightly open at points throughout the half-hour execution. But *AL.com* reported the following: "Alabama Prison Commissioner Jeff Dunn said that the execution went as outlined in the prison system's execution protocol. 'We followed our protocol,' he said... 'The protocol has been approved by the medical community, prison officials and the courts.'"[70]

Rather than preventing unnecessary pain and suffering, these protocols contain arbitrary specificities alongside ambiguous standards and generous grants of discretion. They enable officials to disregard a condemned inmate's evident distress and claim, no matter what transpires, that an execution unfolded in accordance with preestablished benchmarks of humaneness. And in states like Alabama, the state department of corrections does not disclose its execution protocol at all; after the Smith execution, "Dunn declined to provide details of the protocol that the state uses."[71]

While officials point to state protocols in order to say that lethal injection is quality-controlled, those protocols fail to provide any real standard with which the public or the courts can hold state officials accountable. What Denno said in 2002 remained true through the 2010–2020 decade, namely that "The criteria in many protocols are far too vague to assess adequately. When the protocols do offer details, such as the amount and type of chemicals that executioners inject, they oftentimes reveal striking errors and ignorance about the procedure. Such inaccurate or missing information heightens the likelihood that a lethal injection will be botched and suggests that states are not capable of executing an inmate constitutionally."[72]

A CASE STUDY OF CHANGES IN ONE STATE'S LETHAL INJECTION PROTOCOL

To illustrate the cumulative effect of protocol changes over time, the recent history of the death penalty in Ohio provides a very revealing case study. The earliest Ohio lethal injection protocol that we examined is from 2001 and is only seven pages long.[73] The latest, from 2016, is twenty-one pages long.[74] These additional pages, full of complex instructions that demonstrate branching, specificity, discretion, and ambiguity, were added in a piecemeal fashion over the intervening years. In those fifteen years, Ohio's Department of Rehabilitation and Correction promulgated no fewer than sixteen revisions of its lethal injection protocol. Some revisions changed little; others revamped the execution method entirely.

In 2001, the part of the protocol dealing with IV insertion spans about a page. On the topic of IV insertion, the protocol simply reads, "The Execution Team will place the condemned prisoner on the lethal injection bed, secure straps and intravenous injection tubes will then be inserted." The prisoner is allowed to make a final statement before the warden gives a signal to start the execution. The protocol is devoid of instructions about the execution itself, saying only that "the designated members of the execution team will then activate the execution cycle."

After the completion of an execution, the 2001 protocol called for "designated personnel" to examine the prisoner and pronounce them dead. The protocol did not set a specific time limit on the execution, but it did note that the inmate should die as soon as the last drug is injected. The protocol makes no mention of a specific drug cocktail, where to obtain the drugs, how to prepare them, or the necessary qualifications for any person involved in the execution. In its subsequent execution protocols, Ohio replaced all of these omissions with detailed instructions.

Unlike its 2001 protocol, the 2004 version specifies procedures to follow before the execution and some qualifications for various execution officials.[75] A licensed pharmacist must supply the drugs, which are specified: sodium thiopental, pancuronium bromide, and potassium chloride—Chapman's original three-drug cocktail. Executioners are directed to order a "sufficient quantity... as a contingency against the contamination or other inadvertent loss of any of the drugs." Prior to the execution, the inmate must be examined "to establish any unique factors which may impact the manner in which the execution team carries out the execution"—a curious mix of ambiguity and specificity. The protocol also prescribes specific dosages for each drug, which must be prepared by "a person qualified under Ohio law to administer and prepare drugs." However, the protocol is careful to allow exceptions as long as each modification is witnessed, recorded, and provided to those in charge of the execution.

The 2004 protocol was also the first of Ohio's to establish a priority among IV insertion locations. The protocol sets a preference for the "arm veins near the joint between the upper and lower arm." If the executioners are unable to set IV lines there, the protocol allows "a qualified medical person" to select an alternative site anywhere on the body, allowing the invasive cut-down procedure and femoral insertions.

In July 2006, Ohio changed the medical examination and outlined the actual execution in more detail.[76] The protocol anticipates difficulties in IV insertion and mentions them directly:

> Every possible effort shall be made to anticipate and plan for foreseeable difficulties in establishing and maintaining the intravenous (IV) lines. The condemned prisoner shall be evaluated by appropriate trained staff on the day of arrival at the institution, to evaluate the prisoner's veins and plan for the insertion of the IV lines. This evaluation shall include a "hands-on" examination as well as a review of the medical chart. At a minimum, the inmate shall be evaluated upon arrival, later that evening at a time to be determined by the warden, and on the following morning prior to nine a.m. Potential problems shall be noted and discussed, and potential solutions considered, in advance of the execution.

The protocol later directs the execution team to test the IV lines with a small amount of saline and then connect a low-pressure saline drip to the lines before the drug injection. Though the team "shall make every effort to establish IV sites in two locations," there is no clear requirement that they establish two lines. During the execution, the protocol calls for logs of each drug syringe, waiting periods of at least a minute between each drug, and constant monitoring of the IV sites for signs of infiltration (when drugs enter the flesh around an IV line rather than the bloodstream). If both IV insertion sites fail, "the team shall take such time as may be necessary to establish a viable IV site."

These changes, including substantial revisions between the 2001 protocol and the 2004 protocol, indicate that the state was itself aware that issues in earlier lethal injections needed to be addressed and that it believed changes to the protocol would help resolve them. However, the revisions made in 2004 were just the beginning in an ongoing process of revision with little resolution to the problems, indicating that such protocol changes would likely continue to be ineffective.

For example, just a few months after the July 2006 changes, in October 2006, the state made several additional changes. The state's October 2006 protocol omits the 2001 language directing "designated personnel" to examine the body and pronounce death.[77] Unlike prior protocols, this one fails to mention any procedure for determining if the inmate has died and no longer says that the execution should be finished as soon as the last drug is injected. It also requires training sessions for the execution team "no less than once per week" starting thirty days before the execution.

The next protocol update occurred in May 2009.[78] This protocol sets specific topics for the training added in 2006. The topics cover the drugs used in the execution, IV insertion, IV monitoring, and "any legal developments of significance." The protocol also calls for the execution team to include people with "at least one-year experience as a certified medical assistant, phlebotomist, EMT, paramedic, or military corpsman." Its suggestion that the execution team should have people with minimal levels of experience in medical-related areas is an implicit acknowledgment that prior executions could not be well handled by amateurs.

Besides its training requirements, the 2009 protocol calls for certain changes during the execution. First, it directs the team to "roll up the inmate's sleeves" to ensure that the IVs are "plainly visible to persons in the chamber and to those in the equipment room," presumably ensuring that the executioners can detect infiltration. Though the protocol requires the IV site to be visible to the executioners, it need not be visible to witnesses. It also calls for the preparation of two backup syringes of sodium thiopental "for contingent use if the initial IV site fails."

The protocol's most important change involves what happens during the execution itself. It added consciousness checks and the first clear branch in any of Ohio's protocols. After the administration of the sodium thiopental, the protocol directs an executioner to call the inmate's name, shake their shoulder, pinch their arm, or give "some other noxious stimulus" to see if they are conscious. If they are, then the IV site must be checked, and the entire execution started again. The May 2009 protocol also brings back the previous procedure for determining death: "At the completion of the delivery of drugs the curtain will be closed and an appropriate medical professional will evaluate the offender to confirm the fact of his or her death." Unlike the consciousness check, which calls for restarting the procedure if the inmate is still conscious, there is no mention of a contingency plan if the inmate is still alive at the end of the execution.

A few months later, Ohio changed its protocol yet again, this time to accommodate the new one-drug sodium thiopental protocol that it would pioneer.[79] This period coincided with the start of shortages of the drugs that were in Chapman's original drug cocktail, and it illustrates how states were, after years of already needing to regularly redesign their protocols to address problems and potential mishaps, forced to scramble again to make untested changes that would have unpredictable results. This scramble became a regular part of the process of keeping executions going, and it fits with the history of lethal injection's unscientific and haphazard development.

More evidence of this fact is that rather than preparing three drugs, Ohio's November 2009 protocol called for ten syringes of sodium thiopental, each containing one gram of the drug: five for the execution and another five in case anything goes wrong. The protocol also directed the execution team to prepare midazolam and hydromorphone "if the decision is made to use an alternative method," allowing the warden or anyone else in charge to decide on a whim to use an entirely different set of drugs. No state had ever tested either of these drug combinations, and while the one-drug protocol would quickly gain steam with other states, Ohio would not use the two-drug protocol until 2014, when it botched the execution of Dennis McGuire.

The director or the warden was empowered to use this second method at any point during the execution, even after the injection of sodium thiopental—introducing, for the first time in Ohio's protocols, a contingency plan in case the regular procedure does not kill the inmate. If the executioners exercised this option, the protocol directed them to inject the midazolam and hydromorphone into the inmate's muscles rather than through an intravenous line. If this also failed to kill the inmate, the protocol allowed the executioners to administer as many additional doses as they had.

The late 2009 protocol was also Ohio's first to allow for a "sufficient time for death to have occurred" in between the end of the injections and checking for death. Prior protocols either omitted the check, like the October 2006 version, or called for it immediately after the injections finished. Nothing in the November 2009 protocol indicated how long may be "sufficient," giving the state considerable latitude to decide when to end the execution.

The protocol provided similar discretion in its IV insertion directions. While the 2006 protocol permitted executioners to "take the amount of time necessary" to establish two IV sites, the 2009 protocol additionally granted a substantial amount of discretion to the warden:

If the passage of time and the difficulty of the undertaking cause the team members [setting the IV lines] to question the feasibility of establishing two or even one site, the team will consult with the warden. The warden, upon consultation with the Director [of Rehabilitation and Corrections] and others as necessary, will make the decision whether or how long to continue efforts to establish an IV site. The Director shall also consult with legal counsel, the office of the Governor or any others as necessary to discuss the issue and alternatives.

It is unclear from the protocol what these "alternatives" may be beyond the two-drug option. A generous reading of the document suggests that if the team was unable to establish IV sites, the warden might decide to execute the inmate in any way available under state law even if no protocol for that method exists. At the time, Ohio's lethal injection law allowed any combination of drugs that could "quickly and painlessly cause death."[80]

The last of the late 2009 protocol's major changes was the addition of a broad grant of discretion to the warden to make changes "as necessary to ensure that the completion of the execution is carried out in a humane, dignified and professional manner." The protocol anticipated that it would be unable, despite its best efforts, to control what happens in the death chamber. This clause directed the warden, when altering the protocol, to "consider the needs of the condemned inmate, visitors and family members, the execution team, prison staff and others"— a nebulous group that practically allowed the warden to justify any divergence from the written protocol.

The next major change to Ohio's lethal injection protocol came in March 2011, when it switched from sodium thiopental to pentobarbital.[81] This change was made one day before the execution of Johnnie Baston, the first execution by pentobarbital ever conducted. Rather than preparing five grams of sodium thiopental for normal use, the 2011 protocol directed the execution team to prepare two syringes of pentobarbital, 2.5 grams each. Like previous protocols, it also called for an equal number of reserve syringes for use if needed. This protocol retains the two-drug midazolam and hydromorphone backup method introduced in 2009.

A month later, Ohio once again changed its protocol to add language about the visibility of executions.[82] This change came just a day before the state executed Clarence Carter for "stomping... a fellow jail inmate" (Johnny Allen) to death.[83] The new protocol ensured that the inmate's lawyer would always have access to a phone while in the witness room, directed the executioners to close the death chamber's curtains before setting the IV lines, and called for a closed-circuit camera in the chamber so witnesses could see the execution. The protocol also choreographed the careful closing and opening of the curtain while a medical professional checked to see if the inmate had died. The protocol did not clarify when the camera would be turned on and off, simply stating that it must be turned on after the warden finished reading the death warrant.

In September 2011, Ohio changed its protocol yet again, adding five pages to the document.[84] Yet another revision—the third in 2011—indicates that, in fact, Ohio, like other death penalty states, really had no idea how to manage lethal injections in a way that could not be critiqued later for introducing an unacceptable risk of pain and cruelty. For the first time since the 2009 change granting the warden broad discretion over an execution, the 2011 document outlined things that the warden could not vary: the participation of three team members with experience preparing and administering drugs, the drugs themselves, and the functions performed by those qualified team members. The protocol also said, "All Execution Team functions shall be performed by appropriately trained and qualified members of the Execution Team," though it failed to explain what it meant by those vague words.

In addition to restricting the use of discretion, the protocol moved decision-making power from the warden to the director of the Department of Corrections. It reads, "Due to the difficult and sometimes unpredictable nature of the tasks to be performed in carrying out the sentence it may not always be possible to follow these procedures to the letter." In that case, "Only the Director may authorize a deviation from the procedures in this policy directive," and deviations must be documented. Another change clamped down on the warden's discretion to use the secondary two-drug protocol, only allowing it "if execution by IV injection is unfeasible, [...] if pentobarbital [cannot] be obtained," or if the one-drug protocol fails to kill the inmate.

The protocol also made several smaller changes. First, it allowed the warden to appoint a physician as an "auxiliary member of the execution team." Previously, the warden could invite a physician to attend, but prior protocols never treated them as members of the execution team. The designated physician could "provide consultation or advice in the event of some unanticipated circumstance." The protocol did not say if they could step in to help with the execution or set IV lines. The document also clarified that the closed-circuit camera introduced in the previous protocol must stay on during IV insertion even though the curtain remained closed. After the execution is completed, the protocol calls for an "After-Action Review" of all variations, unusual events, and opportunities for improvement.

Despite Ohio's extensive and ongoing efforts to clarify execution procedures and minimize variances, in fact, Ohio's execution team would end up quickly departing from its own protocol, suggesting that the protocols and their extensive revisions would be unable to offset the unpredictable nature and arbitrariness of lethal injection. On November 15, 2011, Ohio executed Reginald Brooks for the fatal shooting of his three sons, Reginald Jr. (seventeen), Vaughn (fifteen), and Niarchos (eleven), in 1982.[85] During the twenty-minute execution, Brooks clenched his hands and held his middle finger up. These movements indicated that something was clearly amiss, and the state, apparently, made decisions at that time that were outside of the protocol.

Although exactly what they did at the time has not been made publicly available, six months later, the Associated Press reported that a federal judge had halted executions because of a deviation from the protocol during the Brooks execution.[86] After the state explained its protocol in court, the judge allowed it to proceed with executions: "[The judge] said the state had narrowly demonstrated it was serious about following its rules. He warned prison officials to get it right the next time." Despite this ruling in the state's favor, based on the evidence of these execution mishaps along with the constant revisions and re-revisions to Ohio's protocols, it is reasonable to wonder whether or not it is even possible to "get it right," at least in a way that will not lead to "getting it wrong" later.

The state would not update its protocol again until October 2013, three months before it botched Dennis McGuire's execution.[87] This time, it updated its drug cocktail to allow an intravenous two-drug protocol of midazolam and hydromorphone. Previously, these drugs could only be used by intramuscular injection.[88] This option, which the warden could select if pentobarbital was unavailable or "deemed unusable by the Medical Team," set the stage for McGuire's execution, when he ended up making choking sounds and several loud snorts and gasps during the injection, as well as convulsing for roughly ten minutes, his eyes rolled to the back of his head, before dying after twenty-four minutes. (Arizona would use the same drug combination that Ohio used for McGuire in the execution of Joseph Wood barely six months later, an execution where, as noted earlier in this chapter, Wood gasped for air for nearly two hours before finally dying.) After McGuire's botched execution, Ohio would not carry out another until 2017.

In the intervening years, Ohio adopted four additional protocols. The last of these is the October 2016 protocol. Figures 17 and 18 display the branching, grants of discretion, careful specificity, and intentional ambiguity that it incorporated. The 2016 protocol is so complicated that we have split it into two parts. Figure 17 covers all of the steps before the drugs flow, and Figure 18 covers everything afterward.

As is the case in some other states, this protocol incorporates three different drug regimes. It allows the warden to select a one-drug protocol with either pentobarbital or sodium thiopental or a three-drug protocol of midazolam, a choice of three different paralytics, and potassium chloride. The protocol does not express a preference for any of these choices, and the warden can choose between them as late as "approximately fourteen (14) days prior to the execution." Once the warden chooses, the protocol requires them to notify the inmate, leaving them only two weeks to respond.

The Ohio story, as it unfolded over the start of the twenty-first century, is hardly a reassuring one for those who looked to lethal injection to allow for execution in an orderly, efficient, and reliable way. And it is more than simply an Ohio story; it is a national story. It is a story of bureaucratic maneuver and adaptation designed to keep

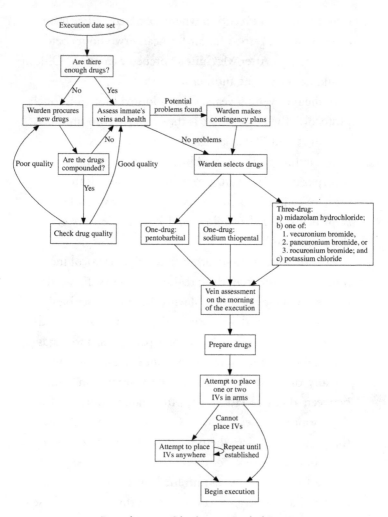

FIGURE 17. Branching in Ohio's 2016 Lethal Injection
Protocol Prior to Injection. (*Source:* Author.)

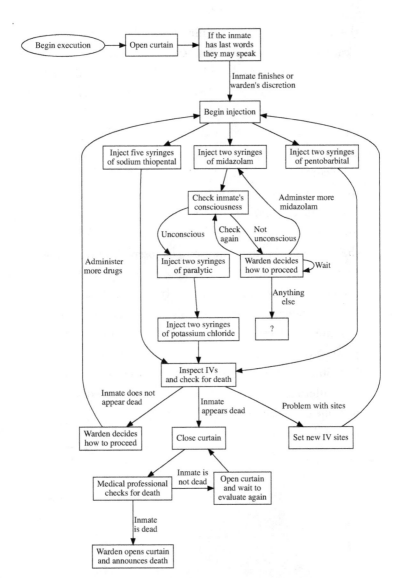

FIGURE 18. Branching in Ohio's 2016 Lethal Injection Protocol after Injection. (*Source:* Author.)

the machinery of death running rather than articulating a clear set of consistent commitments governing the conduct of lethal injection. As the lethal injection paradigm decomposed and as mishaps increased, Ohio and other death penalty states scurried to keep up. They produced incoherent, sometimes even contradictory protocols in rapid succession as they responded to lethal injection's proliferating problems. They tried to stay one step ahead of what courts might require and make lethal injection work in spite of its vexing and continuing problems. They have even "adopted execution protocols for each specific execution, based on the materials available. For example, Joseph Wood was put to death in Arizona on July 23, 2014 under a protocol confirmed by the state on June 25."[89] The frequent, seemingly ad hoc, changes to state protocols have made lethal injection more, not less, haphazard and unpredictable.[90] In this process, death penalty states have neither addressed lethal injection's most serious and recurring defects nor alleviated the suffering of those subject to this supposedly most humane execution method.

6 FAILURE, REFORM, AND THE FUTURE

The recent history of lethal injection recapitulates the trajectory of capital punishment itself. Throughout United States history, when states encountered problems with their methods of execution, they first attempted to address them by tinkering with those methods. When tinkering failed, they adopted allegedly more humane execution methods. When they ran into difficulty with the new methods, state actors scrambled to hide the death penalty's problems from public view.[1] And they have followed this same playbook in the lethal injection era.

During the past decade, states tweaked lethal injection procedures and implemented secrecy measures. Our glimpse into the death chamber—aided by newspaper articles, independent investigations, and court documents—reveals that such changes have done little to make lethal injection more humane.[2] As Deborah Denno puts it: "It is questionable whether any of the [changes to lethal injection procedures]... can fix [them] with a sufficient degree of reliability."[3] In fact, lethal injection became more error-prone as states switched from barbiturate combinations to other types of drug protocols.[4] As the original lethal injection paradigm decomposed, the problems with this method of execution deepened.

Death penalty states responded to lethal injection's problems by resurrecting older methods of execution as backups in case lethal injection becomes "unavailable" in the future. Between 2014 and 2015, six states authorized the firing squad, electrocution, or lethal gas as backup methods of execution, and the federal government joined them in 2020.[5] Today, as noted previously, eight states (Alabama, Arizona, Florida, Kentucky, Mississippi, Oklahoma, South Carolina, and Tennessee) include the electric chair among their available methods of execution. Seven states (Alabama, Arizona, California, Mississippi, Missouri, Oklahoma, and Wyoming) allow for the use of the gas chamber. One, New Hampshire, permits hanging. And four states (Mississippi, Oklahoma, South Carolina, and Utah) authorize the firing squad as an alternative to lethal injection.

Some politicians, including some Republicans, have begun to take stock of the growing evidence of lethal injection's inhumanity and the inability of states to "fix" their way out of it. For example, on December 8, 2020, Ohio's Republican Governor Mike Dewine announced an "unofficial moratorium" on his state's death penalty.[6] The moratorium came almost three years after a federal judge compared Ohio's lethal injection procedure to "waterboarding, suffocation, and exposure to chemical fire." The judge found that lethal injection "will almost certainly subject prisoners to severe pain and needless suffering."[7] Dewine responded that "Ohio is not going to execute someone under my watch when a federal judge has found it to be cruel and unusual punishment." Dewine's comments underscore the fact that Ohio's efforts to keep lethal injection alive over the last twenty years—including switching drug cocktails, adding checks to its procedure, and obscuring mishaps in its death chamber—have not solved its problems. Based on the abundance of evidence about the problems and mishaps associated with lethal injection, it is possible Dewine's actions will in the future become part of a trend away from its use.

Lethal injection's persistent problems remind us of the futility of trying to painlessly and predictably kill humans. As this book has shown, this technology, no matter how advanced it once seemed to be, could not make execution humane. Yet neither abolitionists nor judges have made that fact central to the national conversation about capital punishment. Instead they have devoted most of their attention to the horrendous miscarriages of justice that result in conviction of innocent people for capital crimes they did not commit and to the continuing pattern of arbitrariness and discrimination in death sentencing. It is appropriate that they would attend to those rights violations. But solicitude for the rights of those caught up in this nation's death penalty system should not end at the death house door. The story of lethal injection reminds us that we also need to think about the kind of death that we deliver to those we execute and the fate of the guilty whom the state kills.[8]

Doing so should lead us to revise existing narratives about America's methods of execution.[9] Some have claimed that the evolution of methods of execution in the United States is a story of progress.[10] To them, the adoption of each new execution method marked the abandonment of more barbaric and gruesome methods.[11] But this argument is not supported by the evidence. Indeed, the period from 2010 to 2020 was less a period of progress than of deterioration and decline. New drugs and drug combinations and new procedures may have given the increasingly jerry-rigged lethal injection process a veneer of legitimacy. But none of these recent changes have resolved its fate or repaired its problems.

Looking at its history suggests that lethal injection may have been set up to fail. With its use of IVs, injectable drugs, and EKGs, it resembles a medical procedure. Yet, no execution method can ever live up to medical standards. While doctors are guided by an oath to "do no harm," the executioner's sole goal is to kill.

As Arkansas found out in its 2017 execution spree, nothing can be done to redeem the promise that lethal injection would be this country's most humane execution method. Nothing can be done to rescue it from being the least reliable and most problematic mechanism of state killing. Supreme Court Justice Sonya Sotomayor got it right when she observed, "What cruel irony that the method that appears most humane may turn out to be our most cruel experiment yet."[12] Ending that "cruel experiment" and recognizing the false promise of humane execution should foretell the end of the death penalty itself.

A NOTE ON COLLABORATION

Several years ago, with the support of the Mellon Foundation, Amherst College launched an initiative to encourage research collaborations between students and faculty in the humanities and the humanistic social sciences. For a long time, students interested in the sciences have had the opportunity to do research with faculty. They have worked in labs, analyzed data, attended conferences, and coauthored articles. But until recently there was no parallel for students in other fields. The college's initiative changed things, and this book is a result of that new opportunity for student-faculty collaboration.

In the spring semester of 2020, I offered a research tutorial on America's Death Penalty to six Amherst undergraduates. My goal was to introduce them to the various research traditions that have informed work on capital punishment and equip them to do scholarship in the area. During the semester, I invited my students to work with me on this project on lethal injection. Five of the six students accepted my invitation. Over the next eighteen months, we constructed an archive of the all executions that occurred during the period from 2010 to 2020. The project was designed to carry forward the analysis and argument of my earlier book, *Gruesome Spectacles: Botched Executions and America's Death Penalty*, co-written with another group of Amherst College students.

We developed a conceptual framework and an analysis plan, and reconstructed the history of lethal injection and its rise to prominence as this country's most frequently used execution method. We studied the development and decline of the once standard three-drug cocktail and the consequences of its decline. We identified mishaps that occurred during lethal injections and correlated them with the execution drugs used. Finally, we obtained and analyzed state protocols governing the conduct of executions.

We subsequently presented our work at a meeting of the Law & Society Association and coauthored an article. Over the course of our collaboration the students, whose names appear on the title page of this book, and I met regularly to review the progress of our work, discussed and debated different approaches and interpretations, and exchanged memos and drafts. Our joint efforts extended beyond the graduation from Amherst College of two of the students. Our collaborative work is manifest on every page of this book.

—Austin Sarat

ACKNOWLEDGMENTS

Ours has been an unusual, wonderful collaboration, made possible by financial support from Amherst College. We are grateful for that support. It is unusual for faculty and undergraduate students to write a book together but wonderful to have each other's company as we explored a deeply painful subject.

We also want to express our appreciation to Timothy Kaufman-Osborne, Daniel LaChance, and Susan Shapiro and the anonymous reviewers for helpful comments on earlier iterations of our work. We are also grateful for the interest and enthusiasm of Marcela Cristina Maxfield, our editor at Stanford University Press, and the skilled editorial assistance of Christopher Lura.

Portions of this book previously appeared as "The Fate of Lethal Injection: Decomposition of the Paradigm and Its Consequences," *British Journal of American Legal Studies,* 11 (2022), 3–31.

NOTES

1. This figure was found by taking information from the Death Penalty Information Center about Arkansas's current death row population, subtracting the number of people sentenced since 2017, and adding the number of people executed in 2017. See https://deathpenaltyinfo.org/.

2. "Lethal Injection Procedure (Attachment C)" (Arkansas Department of Corrections, April 11, 2013).

3. Jeannie Nuss, "Arkansas Turns to Different Lethal Injection Drug," *AP News*, April 19, 2013, sec. Prisons, https://apnews.com/article/2dc13f1b27904f18ae322a587c21db99.

4. "Lethal Injection Procedure (Attachment C)" (Arkansas Department of Corrections, August 6, 2015).

5. Ed Pilkington, "'The New Evidence Raises Deeply Troubling Questions': Did Arkansas Kill an Innocent Man?," *The Guardian*, January 23, 2020, http://www.theguardian.com/us-news/2020/jan/23/arkansas-death-penalty-ledell-lee-execution.

6. Eric Besson, John Moritz, and Aziza Musa, "State Carries out 1 Execution," *Arkansas Democrat-Gazette*, April 21, 2017.

7. Previous midazolam executions had been botched and riddled with mishaps. "Witnessing Death: AP Reporters

Describe Problem Executions," *AP News*, April 29, 2017, https://apnews.com/article/bd583ccb99544d9cbe45a60f0afeed55.

8. Ibid.; Eric Besson, Lisa Hammersly, and John Moritz, "2 Killers Executed Hours Apart," *Arkansas Democrat-Gazette*, April 25, 2017.

9. Rolly Hoyt, "Lawmen Recall Jack Jones' Chilling Murder, Rape of Mary Phillips," *THV11*, 2017, https://www.thv11.com/article/news/local/lawmen-recall-jack-jones-chilling-murder-rape-of-mary-phillips/91-433258301.

10. *Jones v. State*, 329 Ark. 62 (1997).

11. Lindsey Millar, "The Jack Jones, Marcel Williams Execution Thread," *Arkansas Times*, April 24, 2017.

12. He developed diabetes in prison and had a leg amputated.

13. Andrew DeMillo and Kelly P. Kissel, "Arkansas Executes Jones," *West Hawaii Today*, April 25, 2017, https://www.westhawaiitoday.com/2017/04/25/nation-world-news/arkansas-executes-jones-plans-2nd-lethal-injection-of-night/.

14. Ed Pilkington, Jamiles Lartey, and Jacob Rosenberg, "Arkansas Carries out First Double Execution in the US for 16 Years," *The Guardian*, April 25, 2017.

15. Besson, Hammersly, and Moritz, "2 Killers Executed Hours Apart."

16. Ibid.

17. Andrew DeMillo and Kelly P. Kissel, "Contrasting Accounts of Arkansas Execution from Witnesses," *AP News*, April 25, 2017.

18. Kelly P. Kissel, "New Issue in Executions: Should the Death Chamber Be Silent?" *Associated Press*, April 25, 2017.

19. DeMillo and Kissel, "Contrasting Accounts of Arkansas Execution from Witnesses."

20. John Moritz, "4 Arkansas Inmates Died of Injection, Recently Completed Reports Show," *Arkansas Democrat-Gazette*, June 8, 2017.

21. Austin Sarat et al., *Gruesome Spectacles: Botched Executions and America's Death Penalty* (Stanford, CA: Stanford University Press, 2014).

22. Michel Foucault, *Discipline and Punish* (New York: Vintage Press, 1977).

23. Susan Blaustein, "Witness to Another Execution," *Harper's Magazine*, May 1994; Richard Trombley, *The Execution Protocol: Inside America's Capital Punishment Industry* (New York: Crown, 1992).

24. Allen Huang, "Hanging, Cyanide Gas, and the Evolving Standards of Decency: The Ninth Circuit's Misapplication of the Cruel and Unusual Clause of the Eighth Amendment," *Oregon Law Review* 74 (1995): 995.

25. Several scholars have discussed the history of the death penalty and its medicalization, sterilization, and privatization. For example, Deborah Denno has written extensively on the medical appearances associated with lethal injection, as well as the changes in middle-class culture in the twentieth century that left citizens in search of cleaner, more humane methods of execution. "The Lethal Injection Quandary: How Medicine Has Dismantled the Death Penalty," *Fordham Law Review* 76, no. 1 (2007): 49–128. In addition, Stuart Banner writes that the early twentieth century saw "the continual centralization and professionalization of punishment" and the development of new technologies of execution. *The Death Penalty: An American History* (Cambridge, MA: Harvard University Press, 2002), 505.

26. Robert Johnson, *Death Work: A Study of the Modern Execution Process* (Pacific Grove, CA: Brooks/Cole, 1990). See also Thomas Metzger, *Blood and Volts: Edison, Tesla, and the Electric Chair* (Brooklyn, NY: Autonomedia, 1996).

27. *Hill v. Lockhart*, 791 F. Supp. 1388 (E.D. Ark. 1992). See also *Ex Parte Kenneth Granviel*, 561 S.W. 2d 503, 513 (Tex. Crim. App. 1978). The court found that "the Texas Legislature

substituted death by lethal injection as a means of execution in lieu of electrocution for the reason it would be a more humane and less spectacular form of execution." And as Justice Anstead argued in *Provenzano v. Moore*, 744 So. 2d 413, 446 (Fla. 1999), "Just as electrocution may have been originally evaluated in comparison with hanging, we know today that the overwhelming majority of death penalty jurisdictions have long since rejected use of the electric chair and have turned to lethal injection as a more humane punishment."

28. Abernethy argues that "contrary to what logic seems to dictate, the attempt over time has been to make the penalty of death gentle, hidden, and antiseptic." Jonathan S. Abernethy, "The Methodology of Death: Reexamining the Deterrence Rationale," *Columbia Human Rights Law Review* 27, no. 2 (January 1, 1996): 422.

29. "Death Penalty," *Gallup*, 2021, https://news.gallup.com/poll/1606/Death-Penalty.aspx. This response compared with 9 percent for the firing squad, 5 percent for hanging, and 4 percent each for the electric chair and the gas chamber. 10 percent said that no method of execution should be called humane.

30. Sarat et al., *Gruesome Spectacles*.

31. Pilkington, Lartey, and Rosenberg, "Arkansas Carries out First Double Execution in the US for 16 Years."

32. Frank E. Lockwood, "Arkansas Jurors Were Never Told of Marcel Williams' Life; Grave Error, Judge Said," *Arkansas Democrat-Gazette*, April 24, 2017, https://www.arkansasonline.com/news/2017/apr/25/jurors-were-never-told-of-williams-life/.

33. Fiona Keating, "Judge Orders Blood and Tissue Samples from Botched Arkansas Execution Body for Autopsy," *International Business Times*, April 30, 2017, https://www.ibtimes.co.uk/judge-orders-blood-tissue-samples-botched-arkansas-execution-body-autopsy-1619352.

34. Jacob Rosenberg, "Arkansas Executions: 'I Was Watching Him Breathe Heavily and Arch His Back,'" *The Guardian*,

April 25, 2017, http://www.theguardian.com/us-news/2017/apr/25/arkansas-execution-eyewitness-marcel-williams.

35. Kissel, "New Issue in Executions: Should the Death Chamber Be Silent?"

36. Keating, "Judge Orders Blood and Tissue Samples from Botched Arkansas Execution Body for Autopsy."

37. Erika Ferrando and Kaitlin Barger, "Kenneth Williams, Convicted Murderer of UAPB Cheerleader, to Be Executed Thursday," *THV 11*, April 28, 2017, https://www.thv11.com/article/news/local/kenneth-williams-convicted-murderer-of-uapb-cheerleader-to-be-executed-thursday/91-434214516.

38. Ibid.

39. Olivia Messer, "Gangster by 9, Murderer by 19, Minister by 26. Executed by 39?," *Daily Beast*, April 17, 2017, sec. us-news, https://www.thedailybeast.com/articles/2017/04/17/gangster-by-9-murderer-by-19-minister-by-26-executed-by-39.

40. Ibid.

41. Liliana Segura, "Arkansas Justice: Racism, Torture, and a Botched Execution," *The Intercept*, November 12, 2017, https://theintercept.com/2017/11/12/arkansas-death-row-executions-kenneth-williams/.

42. In 1913, Arkansas switched from hanging to electrocution. Ibid.

43. Segura, "Arkansas Justice: Racism, Torture, and a Botched Execution."

44. Phil McCausland, "Arkansas Execution of Kenneth Williams 'Horrifying': Lawyer," *NBC News*, April 27, 2017, https://www.nbcnews.com/storyline/lethal-injection/arkansas-executes-kenneth-williams-4th-lethal-injection-week-n752086.

45. Ibid.

46. Linda Satter, "In Court, Expert Doubts Arkansas Execution Drug's Efficacy," *Arkansas Democrat-Gazette*, April 24, 2019.

47. McCausland, "Arkansas Execution of Kenneth Williams 'Horrifying': Lawyer."

48. Andrew DeMillo, "Federal Judge Upholds Use of Sedative in Arkansas Executions," *AP News*, June 2, 2020, https://apnews.com/article/c3bdd9dc861f99d24aaceba12569fbb2.

49. Quoted in Elizabeth Weil, "The Needle and the Damage Done," *New York Times,* February 11, 2007, https://www.nytimes.com/2007/02/11/magazine/11injection.t.html

50. Ibid.

51. Eric Berger, "The Executioners' Dilemmas," *University of Richmond Law Review* 49 (2015), 735.

52. This formulation was suggested by one of the anonymous reviewers of this manuscript.

CHAPTER 2

1. Robert Hoag, "Capital Punishment," in *Internet Encyclopedia of Philosophy*, accessed October 30, 2021, https://iep.utm.edu/cap-puni/.

2. Frank E. Grizzard Jr. and D. Boyd Smith, *Jamestown Colony: A Political, Social, and Cultural History* (ABC-CLIO, 2007), 109.

3. "Early History of the Death Penalty," *Death Penalty Information Center*, accessed October 29, 2021, https://deathpenalty info.org/facts-and-research/history-of-the-death-penalty/early -history-of-the-death-penalty.

4. Stuart Banner, *The Death Penalty: An American History* (Cambridge, MA: Harvard University Press, 2002).

5. Austin Sarat et al., *Gruesome Spectacles: Botched Executions and America's Death Penalty* (Stanford, CA: Stanford University Press, 2014).

6. Lawrence M. Friedman, *Crime and Punishment in American History* (New York: Basic Books, 1993).

7. Elbridge T. Gerry, Alfred P. Southwick, and Matthew Hale, *Report of the Commission to Investigate and Report the*

Most Humane and Practical Method of Carrying into Effect the Sentence of Death in Capital Cases (The Troy Press Company, 1888), 63, http://hdl.handle.net/2027/coo.31924072059565.

8. Gerry, Southwick, and Hale, *Report of the Commission.*

9. Ibid.

10. "Instead of acting as a deterrent, public hangings tended to celebrate crime and glorify the criminal. The opportunity for the condemned man to display courage and valor by walking steadily from his jail cell to the scaffold only added to his exalted status." Richard Moran, *Executioner's Current: Thomas Edison, George Westinghouse, and the Invention of the Electric Chair* (New York: Vintage Books, 2003), 82.

11. Gerry, Southwick, and Hale, *Report of the Commission.*

12. Martin Pernick, *A Calculus of Suffering: Pain, Professionalism, and Anesthesia in Nineteenth-Century America* (New York: Columbia University Press, 1985).

13. Timothy V. Kaufman-Osborn, *From Noose to Needle: Capital Punishment and the Late Liberal State, Law, Meaning, and Violence* (Ann Arbor: University of Michigan Press, 2002).

14. Pernick, *A Calculus of Suffering.*

15. Kaufman-Osborn, *From Noose to Needle.*

16. Gerry, Southwick, and Hale, *Report of the Commission.*

17. "Elbridge T. Gerry Papers, 1856–1912," *Columbia University Libraries Archival Collections*, accessed October 29, 2021, http://www.columbia.edu/cu/lweb/archival/collections/ldpd_4078804/.

18. Elbridge T. Gerry, "Capital Punishment by Electricity," *North American Review* 149, no. 394 (1889): 321–25.

19. Gerry, Southwick, and Hale, *Report of the Commission*, 80.

20. Ibid., 76–80.

21. J. Mount Bleyer, "Best Method of Executing Criminals," *Medico-Legal Journal* 5, no. 1 (1888): 429, https://archive.org/details/medicolegaljourno5medi/page/424.

22. Gerry, Southwick, and Hale, *Report of the Commission*, 76, 82.

23. Moran, *Executioner's Current*, 110. It is worth noting that one very influential electrician favored the electric chair. Thomas Edison advocated for an electric chair using alternating current (AC). Edison's support of the chair stemmed from his desire to tarnish his rival's reputation. An AC electric chair would, he hoped, drive customers away from Westinghouse's AC products and toward Edison's direct current (DC) products.

24. Gerry, Southwick, and Hale, *Report of the Commission*, 90.

25. Robert Craig, "A History of Syringes and Needles," *University of Queensland Faculty of Medicine*, December 20, 2018, https://medicine.uq.edu.au/blog/2018/12/history-syringes-and-needles.

26. "Origin of the Hypodermic Needle," *TMR International Hospital*, October 22, 2019, https://tmrinternational.org/when-was-the-needle-was-invented/.

27. "Mrs. Wharton's Defence," *New York Herald*, December 31, 1871, Library of Congress; "Slaves to a Fatal Habit," *Savannah Morning News*, September 14, 1884, Library of Congress; "The Effect of Alcohol," *Sacramento Daily Record-Union*, July 2, 1886, Library of Congress; "Deadly Drug Deals," *Salt Lake Herald*, June 10, 1888, Library of Congress; "The Hypodermic Needle," *Oskaloosa Herald*, July 9, 1885, Library of Congress.

28. Bleyer, "Best Method of Executing Criminals."

29. Ibid., 437.

30. Moran, *Executioner's Current*, 73.

31. Bleyer, "Best Method of Executing Criminals," 435; Moran, *Executioner's Current*, 73.

32. Moran, *Executioner's Current*, 73; Bleyer, "Best Method of Executing Criminals," 437.

33. Bleyer, "Best Method of Executing Criminals," 436.

34. Ibid., 435–36; Moran, *Executioner's Current*, 73.

35. Bleyer, "Best Method of Executing Criminals," 437.

36. Ibid., 441; Moran, *Executioner's Current*, 73–79.

37. Moran, *Executioner's Current*, 79.

38. *Gregg v. Georgia*, 428 U.S. 153 (1976). For discussions of *Gregg*, see Linda Katherine Richey, "Death Penalty Statutes: A Post-Gregg v. Georgia Survey and Discussion of Eighth Amendment Safeguards," *Washburn Law Journal* 16, no. 2 (1977): 497–515; Hugo Adam Bedau, "Gregg v. Georgia and the 'New' Death Penalty," *Criminal Justice Ethics* 4, no. 2 (June 1, 1985): 3–17, doi:10.1080/0731129X.1985.9991777; Hugo Adam Bedau, *The Death Penalty in America* (Oxford University Press, 1998); Linda J. Norris, "Constitutional Law—The Death Penalty as Punishment for the Crime of Murder Does Not Violate the Eighth Amendment," *Texas Tech Law Review* 8, no. 2 (1976): 515–23.

39. *Furman v. Georgia*, 408 U.S. 238 (1972).

40. *Gregg*, 428 U.S. at 164–67.

41. Ibid., at 158–59.

42. Ibid., at 227–41.

43. Ibid., at 169.

44. Von Russell Creel, "Capital Punishment," in *The Encyclopedia of Oklahoma History and Culture* (Oklahoma Historical Society), accessed January 29, 2021, https://www.okhistory.org/publications/enc/entry.php?entry=CA052; "Gov. David Lyle Boren," *National Governors Association*, 2021, https://www.nga.org/governor/david-lyle-boren/.

45. *B26 R7 S2*, MP3 audio, Senate Proceedings, Taped, 1977, Oklahoma Department of Libraries Archives and Records Division.

46. John Greiner, "State's Politicians Rally in Seminole to Honor Bill Dawson," *The Oklahoman*, May 29, 1986, https://oklahoman.com/article/2148993/states-politicians-rally-in-seminole-to-honor-bill-dawson/.

47. "Oklahoma Man Who Developed Lethal Injection Recipe Lived with Regret," *News on 6*, May 1, 2014, https://www.newson6.com/story/5e3631ea2f69d76f62051033/oklahoma-man-who-developed-lethal-injection-recipe-lived-with-regret.

48. *B26 R7 S2*.

49. Vince Beiser, "A Guilty Man," *Mother Jones*, September/October 2005, https://www.motherjones.com/politics/2005/09/guilty-man/. The British Royal Commission on Capital Punishment (1949–1953) also considered adopting lethal injection, but the commission concluded that "human nature is so constituted as to make it easier for a condemned man to show courage and composure in his last moments if the final act required of him is a positive one, such as walking to the scaffold, than if it is mere passivity, like awaiting the prick of a needle." Dick Reavis, "Charlie Brooks' Last Words," *Texas Monthly*, February 1, 1983, https://www.texasmonthly.com/articles/charlie-brooks-last-words/.

50. Lethal injection was also rejected in Britain because of the strong objections of the British Medical Society. Melvin F. Wingersky, "Report of the Royal Commission on Capital Punishment (1949–1953): A Review," *Journal of Criminal Law, Criminology, and Police Science* 44, no. 6 (1954): 705.

51. Ziva Branstetter, "'Father of Lethal Injection' Talks about History, His Legacy to Oklahoma," *Tulsa World*, February 13, 2019, https://tulsaworld.com/news/state-and-regional/father-of-lethal-injection-talks-about-history-his-legacy-to-oklahoma/article_0bb18eb4-7706-524a-8bf0-00a4f6117fa7.html.

52. Deborah W. Denno, "The Lethal Injection Quandary: How Medicine Has Dismantled the Death Penalty," *Fordham Law Review* 76, no. 1 (2007): 66.

53. Ibid., 66–67.

54. "So Long as They Die: Lethal Injections in the United States," Human Rights Watch, April 23, 2006, https://www.hrw.org/report/2006/04/23/so-long-they-die/lethal-injections-united-states.

. 55. Denno, "The Lethal Injection Quandary," 66–67. Chapman's proposal was, however, reviewed and endorsed by an anesthesiologist named Stanley Deutsch.

56. "Senate Sponsors Push Execution by Drugs Bill," *Salpulpa Daily Herald*, March 3, 1977, Oklahoma Historical Society, https://gateway.okhistory.org/ark:/67531/metadc1495069/.

57. *B26 R9 S2*, MP3 audio, Senate Proceedings, Taped, 1977, Oklahoma Department of Libraries Archives and Records Division.

58. *B26 R7 S2*; John Greiner and Randy Ellis, "Former Oklahoma State Sen. Gene Stipe Dies at 85," *The Oklahoman*, July 21, 2012, https://www.oklahoman.com/article/3694504/former-oklahoma-state-sen-gene-stipe-dies-at-85. Stipe, who spent fifty-three years in the State Senate, was the longest serving Oklahoma state senator. He stepped down in 2003 after pleading guilty to federal campaign violations.

59. *B26 R7 S2*.

60. Ibid.

61. Denno, "The Lethal Injection Quandary," 74.

62. "So Long as They Die."

63. Ibid.

64. *B26 R9 S2*.

65. Jonathan R. Sorensen and Rocky LeAnn Pilgrim, *Lethal Injection: Capital Punishment in Texas during the Modern Era*, 1st ed. (University of Texas Press, 2006), 9.

66. Ibid., 10.

67. "Executions Could Come through Lethal Injection," *Hereford Brand*, April 22, 1977, https://newspaperarchive.com/politics-clipping-apr-22-1977-1776741/.

68. Sorensen and Pilgrim, *Lethal Injection*, 11.

69. "House Study Group Bill Analysis of HB 945," Texas House of Representatives Committee on Criminal Jurisprudence, 1977.

70. Sorensen and Pilgrim, *Lethal Injection*, 11.

71. "Execution Opponents Seek Moratorium," *Lubbock Avalanche-Journal*, February 28, 1977.

72. "Criminal Procedure—Death Sentence—Methods of Inflicting," Pub. L. No. 41, 22 Ok. St. § 1014 (1977); "Execution Method of Convicts Sentenced to Death," Pub. L. No. 138, Tex. Crim. Proc. § 43.14 (1977).

73. James Welsh, "The Medical Technology of Execution: Lethal Injection," *International Review of Law, Computers & Technology* 12, no. 1 (1998): 7.

74. Idaho in 1978, New Mexico in 1979, and Washington in 1981.

75. "Criminal Procedure—Death Sentence—Methods of Inflicting."

76. "Infliction of Death Penalty," Idaho Code § 19-2716 (1978).

77. "Punishment of Death; How Inflicted," N.M. Stat. § 31-14-11 (1979).

78. According to the Death Penalty Information Center, Idaho executed three inmates with lethal injection, New Mexico executed one, and Washington executed five. "Execution Database," Death Penalty Information Center, January 16, 2021, https://deathpenaltyinfo.org/executions/execution-database.

79. Ibid.

80. Reavis, "Charlie Brooks' Last Words"; Robert Reinhold, "Technician Executes Murderer in Texas by Lethal Injection," *New York Times*, December 7, 1982, https://www.nytimes.com/1982/12/07/us/technician-executes-murderer-in-texas-by-lethal-injection.html.

81. Reavis, "Charlie Brooks' Last Words."

82. Prison guards strapped Kemmler into the electric chair, covered his face, and shot 1,000 volts of electric current through his body for seventeen seconds. His body writhed and caught fire, but he continued to breathe heavily, his chest

expanding and contracting as drool fell down his chin. The warden ordered a second wave of current. This time, 2,000 volts of electricity went through Kemmler for seventy-three seconds, causing his blood vessels to rupture. In stark contrast to the quick and humane death that the new technology promised, Kemmler's electrocution was torturously long and filled the chamber with the odor of burning flesh. See Michael S. Rosenwald, "'Great God, He Is Alive!' The First Man Executed by Electric Chair Died Slower Than Thomas Edison Expected," *Washington Post*, April 28, 2017, https://www.washingtonpost .com/news/retropolis/wp/2017/04/26/thomas-edison-the-electric -chair-and-a-botched-execution-a-death-penalty-primer/.

83. Reavis, "Charlie Brooks' Last Words."

84. Don Colburn, "Lethal Injection," *Washington Post*, December 11, 1990, https://www.washingtonpost.com/archive/ lifestyle/wellness/1990/12/11/lethal-injection/5838a159-cd73 -440e-a208-850d318be8fe/; Reinhold, "Technician Executes Murderer in Texas by Lethal Injection."

85. Reavis, "Charlie Brooks' Last Words."

86. Ibid.

87. "The Death Penalty in Massachusetts: Facts and History," *NODP*, March 1, 2008, accessed October 29, 2021, http://www.nodp.org/ma/s1.html.

88. Nick King, "Doctors Debate Ethics of Death by Injection," *Boston Globe*, December 8, 1982.

89. Ibid.

90. Chris Black, "Execution Unlikely for Years; Mass. Bill Requires a Lengthy Process before Anyone Is Put to Death," *Boston Globe*, December 16, 1982.

91. Ibid. Claus von Bülow was a Danish-born lawyer and socialite who was initially convicted for murdering his heiress wife but was later acquitted after hiring Harvard Law Professor Alan Dershowitz and eight university professors as medical

experts. Enid Nemy, "Claus von Bülow, Society Figure in High-Profile Case, Dies at 92," *New York Times*, May 30, 2019, sec. Obituaries.

92. Deborah W. Denno, "Lethal Injection Chaos Post-Baze," *Georgetown Law Journal* 102, no. 5 (2013): 1341.

93. "Method of Execution," Pub. L. No. 774, Ark. C. Ann. § 5-4-167 (1983).

94. Nathaniel R. Code Jr., "Excerpt from Petitioner's Post-Hearing Memorandum," 2015, 20, https://www.clearinghouse.net/chDocs/public/CJ-LA-0001-0007.pdf.

95. Ibid.

96. "So Long as They Die."

97. Code, "Excerpt from Petitioner's Post-Hearing Memorandum."

98. Ibid., 12.

99. Code, "Excerpt from Petitioner's Post-Hearing Memorandum."

100. "So Long as They Die."

101. Charles R. Shipan and Craig Volden, "Policy Diffusion: Seven Lessons for Scholars and Practitioners," *Public Administration Review* 72, no. 6 (2012): 790.

102. Kurt Weyland, "Theories of Policy Diffusion: Lessons from Latin American Pension Reform," *World Politics* 57, no. 2 (2005): 262–95.

103. Ira Sharkansky and Richard I. Hofferbert, "Dimensions of State Politics, Economics, and Public Policy," *American Political Science Review* 63, no. 3 (2014): 879, doi:10.1017/S0003055400258632.

104. *New State Ice Co. v. Liebmann*, 285 U.S. 262 (1932).

105. As Chapman himself explained, "'The idea of testing these drugs, it's just a ridiculous notion as far as I'm concerned.'" Quoted in Josh Sanburn, "The 'Father of Lethal Injection' Says the Method Is Still Humane If Done Properly,"

Time, May 15, 2014, https://time.com/101143/lethal-injection
-creator-jay-chapman-botched-executions/.

106. Corinna Barrett Lain, "Death Penalty Exceptionalism
and Administrative Law," *Belmont Law Review* 8, no. 2 (2020):
566.

107. Ibid.

CHAPTER 3

1. *Baze v. Rees*, 553 U.S. 35 (2008).

2. Molly E. Grace, "Baze v. Rees: Merging Eighth Amendment Precedents into a New Standard for Method of Execution Challenges," *Maryland Law Review* 68, no. 2 (2009): 436.

3. *Baze*, 553 U.S. at 52.

4. Ibid., at 57.

5. Grace, "Baze v. Rees," 430. This standard, promulgated
by the plurality of the court in *Baze*, became the basis for the
majority opinion in *Glossip v. Gross*, 135 S.Ct. 2726 (2015). In
Glossip, petitioners challenged Oklahoma's midazolam lethal
injection protocol. The court held that the protocol was permissible for the same reasons as Kentucky's use of the traditional three-drug protocol challenged in *Baze*. Nowadays, the
requirement that inmates present a readily available alternative
method that significantly reduces a substantial risk of severe
pain is known as the *Glossip* doctrine.

6. Deborah W. Denno, "Lethal Injection Chaos Post-Baze,"
Georgetown Law Journal 102, no. 5 (2013): 1354.

7. The new protocol was the same as the one that Ralph
Baze and Thomas Bowling had proposed in *Baze v. Rees*.

8. Denno, "Lethal Injection Chaos Post-Baze," 1358–60.

9. For a discussion of this argument see Eric Berger "Evolving Standards of Lethal Injection," in *The Eighth Amendment
and Its Future in a New Age of Punishment*, ed. Meghan Ryan

and William Berry (New York: Cambridge University Press, 2020). Also Deborah Denno, "Back to the Future with Execution Methods," in *The Eighth Amendment and Its Future in a New Age of Punishment*, ed. Meghan Ryan and William Berry (New York: Cambridge University Press, 2020).

10. James Gibson and Corinna Barrett Lain, "Death Penalty Drugs and the International Moral Marketplace," *Georgetown Law Journal* 103, no. 5 (2015): 1221; "Pfizer Completes Acquisition of Hospira," *Pfizer*, September 3, 2015, https://www.pfizer.com/news/press-release/press-release-detail/pfizer_completes_acquisition_of_hospira; Jeffrey E. Stern, "The Cruel and Unusual Execution of Clayton Lockett," *The Atlantic*, June 2015, https://www.theatlantic.com/magazine/archive/2015/06/execution-clayton-lockett/392069/.

11. Matthew C. Bergs, "Execution by . . . Heroin?: Why States Should Challenge the FDA's Ban on the Importation of Sodium Thiopental," *Iowa Law Review* 102 (2017): 761.

12. Gibson and Lain, "Death Penalty Drugs and the International Moral Marketplace," 1222.

13. Sean Murphy, "Man Apologizes to Victim's Family," *The Oklahoman*, December 17, 2010.

14. In general, we do not distinguish drug protocols that switch their second and third drugs for close analogues that have the same intended effect when injected. For example, states sometimes substitute vecuronium bromide or rocuronium bromide for pancuronium bromide, as is the case here. With a few exceptions, it is very difficult to determine exactly which second and third drugs a state used in a given execution since newspapers commonly report the first drug but not the others. Furthermore, execution procedures often allow choices between similar second and third drugs.

15. Gibson and Lain, "Death Penalty Drugs and the International Moral Marketplace," 1223.

16. Raymond Bonner, "Drug Company in Cross Hairs of Death Penalty Opponents," *New York Times*, March 30, 2011, https://www.nytimes.com/2011/03/31/world/europe/31iht-letter 31.html.

17. Gibson and Lain, "Death Penalty Drugs and the International Moral Marketplace," 1225.

18. Mary D. Fan, "The Supply-Side Attack on Lethal Injection and the Rise of Execution Secrecy," *Boston University Law Review* 95, no. 2 (2015): 427–60.

19. Eric Berger, "Courts, Culture, and the Lethal Injection Stalemate," *William and Mary Law Review* 62 (2020): 1

20. Ibid., 33.

21. Ibid., 1.

22. Owen Dyer, "The Slow Death of Lethal Injection," *British Medical Journal* 348 (April 29, 2014), https://www.jstor.org/stable/26514666; Denno, "Lethal Injection Chaos Post-Baze," 1361.

23. "Britain to Ban Export to U.S. of Execution Drugs," *Reuters*, April 15, 2011, sec. Health, https://www.reuters.com/article/us-britain-execution-drugs-idINTRE73E4WQ20110415.

24. Gibson and Lain, "Death Penalty Drugs and the International Moral Marketplace," 1226.

25. The states were Oklahoma, Texas, South Carolina, Mississippi, Alabama, Arizona, Georgia, Delaware, Virginia, Florida, Idaho, and Ohio.

26. Protocols allowed for even more novel drug combinations, like midazolam and hydromorphone, as backups.

27. "Ohio Turns to Untried Execution Drug Mix Due to Shortage of Pentobarbital," *The Guardian*, October 28, 2013, http://www.theguardian.com/world/2013/oct/28/ohio-untried-execution-drugs-pentobarbital-shortage.

28. David Jolly, "Danish Company Blocks Sale of Drug for U.S. Executions," *New York Times*, July 1, 2011, https://www.nytimes.com/2011/07/02/world/europe/02execute.html.

29. Gibson and Lain, "Death Penalty Drugs and the International Moral Marketplace," 1229.

30. Dyer, "The Slow Death of Lethal Injection"; Ross Levitt and Deborah Feyerick, "Death Penalty States Scramble for Lethal Injection Drugs," *CNN*, November 15, 2013, https://www.cnn.com/2013/11/15/justice/states-lethal-injection-drugs/index.html.

31. "Arizona DoC Paid $1.5 Million for Execution Drugs While Facing a Budget Crisis," *Death Penalty Information Center*, April 15, 2021, https://deathpenaltyinfo.org/news/arizona-doc-paid-1-5-million-for-execution-drugs-while-facing-a-budget-shortfall.

32. "Overview of Lethal Injection Protocols," *Death Penalty Information Center*, accessed October 29, 2021, https://deathpenaltyinfo.org/executions/lethal-injection/overview-of-lethal-injection-protocols.

33. Denno, "Lethal Injection Chaos Post-Baze," 1376.

34. Gabrielle Emanuel, "5 Things You Need To Know About the New England Compounding Center Trial," *GBH News*, March 21, 2017, sec. Local, https://www.wgbh.org/news/2017/03/21/local-news/5-things-you-need-know-about-new-england-compounding-center-trial; "Former Owner of Defunct New England Compounding Center Resentenced to 14 Years in Prison in Connection with 2012 Fungal Meningitis Outbreak" (District of Massachusetts U.S. Attorney, July 7, 2021), https://www.justice.gov/usao-ma/pr/former-owner-defunct-new-england-compounding-center-resentenced-14-years-prison.

35. For those acts, Barry Cadden, the former owner of NECC, was sentenced to fourteen years in prison, fined more than a million dollars, and ordered to pay over $82 million in restitution.

36. "Compounding Pharmacies and Lethal Injection," *Death Penalty Information Center*, accessed September 25, 2021,

https://deathpenaltyinfo.org/executions/lethal-injection/compounding-pharmacies.

37. Steve Young, "Execution: South Dakota Delivers Eric Robert His Death Wish," *Argus Leader*, October 16, 2012.

38. Breathing changes like gasping and snoring are possible signs of pulmonary edema, which we discuss below.

39. Young, "Execution: South Dakota Delivers Eric Robert His Death Wish."

40. Clare Dyer, "WMA Says Doctors Must Not Prescribe Drugs for Execution," *British Medical Journal* 345 (October 19, 2012), doi:10.1136/bmj.e7076.

41. Terri Langford, Alex Duner, and Jessica Hamel, "Timeline: A History of Lethal Drug Use in Texas," *Texas Tribune*, July 8, 2014, https://www.texastribune.org/2014/07/08/history-lethal-drug-use-texas/.

42. Rick Thaler, "Execution Procedure" (Texas Department of Criminal Justice Correctional Institutions Division, July 9, 2012), 8, https://web.archive.org/web/20210820003453/https://s3.amazonaws.com/graphics.texastribune.org/dailies/graphics/execution-drugs-timeline/src/TDCJ%20Execution%20Protocol%2007-09-2012%20Final.pdf.

43. Langford, Duner, and Hamel, "Timeline: A History of Lethal Drug Use in Texas."

44. "Death Row Information: Yowell, Michael J.," *Texas Department of Criminal Justice*, accessed October 29, 2021, https://www.tdcj.texas.gov/death_row/dr_info/yowellmichael.html.

45. Langford, Duner, and Hamel, "Timeline: A History of Lethal Drug Use in Texas."

46. Walt Nett, "Yowell Tells Executioner: 'Punch the Button,'" *Lubbock Avalanche-Journal*, October 9, 2013.

47. Barri Dean, "What Are Those Ingredients You Are Mixing Up behind Your Veil," *Howard Law Journal* 62, no. 1 (2018): 316.

48. Ibid., 317.

49. Ibid., 321.

50. Gibson and Lain, "Death Penalty Drugs and the International Moral Marketplace," 1234.

51. Kelly A. Mennemeier, "A Right to Know How You'll Die: A First Amendment Challenge to State Secrecy Statutes Regarding Lethal Injection Drugs," *Journal of Criminal Law and Criminology* 107, no. 3 (2017): 453.

52. Formerly known as the International Academy of Compounding Pharmacists.

53. Gibson and Lain, "Death Penalty Drugs and the International Moral Marketplace," 1235.

54. Just as we do not typically distinguish between protocols that use close analogues in the second or third drugs, we do not distinguish between protocols using midazolam and those using midazolam hydrochloride.

55. Morgan Watkins, "Happ Executed Using New Drug," *Gainsville Sun*, October 15, 2013.

56. Bill Cotterell, "Florida Executes Man with New Lethal Injection Drug," *Reuters*, October 15, 2013, https://www.reuters.com/article/usa-florida-execution-idINL1N0I521020131015.

57. "Lacking Lethal Injection Drugs, States Find Untested Backups," *NPR*, October 26, 2013, https://www.npr.org/2013/10/26/241011316/lacking-lethal-injection-drugs-states-find-untested-backups.

58. Hydromorphone had never been used in a lethal injection. The federal court that approved the first execution with Ohio's new protocol wrote, "There is absolutely no question that Ohio's current protocol presents an experiment in lethal injection processes." *In re Ohio Execution Protocol Litig.*, 994 F. Supp. 2d 906 (S.D. Ohio 2014).

59. Lawrence Hummer, "I Witnessed Ohio's Execution of Dennis McGuire. What I Saw Was Inhumane," *The Guardian*,

June 14, 2014; Josh Sweigart, "Ohio Executes McGuire, Killer of Preble County Woman in 1989," *Dayton Daily News*, January 16, 2014, https://www.daytondailynews.com/news/local/ohio-executes-mcguire-killer-preble-county-woman-1989/ddQzdQpjWlwl9q4pir9oEL/.

60. Andrew Welsh-Huggins, "Ohio Killer Executed with New Lethal Drug Combo," *AP News*, January 16, 2014.

61. The appeal was denied by Supreme Court Justice Anthony Kennedy, but the decision did not come before Wood was pronounced dead.

62. Lesley M. Williams, Katharine L. Boyd, and Brian M. Fitzgerald, "Etomidate," in *StatPearls* (Treasure Island, FL: StatPearls Publishing, 2021), http://www.ncbi.nlm.nih.gov/books/NBK535364/; Jeffrey L. Giese and Theodore H. Stanley, "Etomidate: A New Intravenous Anesthetic Induction Agent," *Pharmacotherapy: The Journal of Human Pharmacology and Drug Therapy* 3, no. 5 (September 10, 1983): 251–58, doi:10.1002/j.1875-9114.1983.tb03266.x.

63. Josh Sanburn, "Oklahoma's Lethal Injection Problems Go from Bad to Worse," *Time*, October 8, 2015, https://time.com/4067071/oklahoma-lethal-injection-wrong-drug-charles-warner/. Oklahoma made this error in the execution of Charles Warner, who was sentenced to death for the rape and murder of an eleven-month-old. A service log filled out on the day of the execution records that the last two syringes administered to Warner were filled with "120 mEq Potassium Chloride." The autopsy found, however, that the drug was mislabeled: the syringes' contents had actually been potassium acetate. When the drugs began flowing, Warner said, "My body is on fire." Eyder Peralta, "Oklahoma Used the Wrong Drug to Execute Charles Warner," *NPR*, October 8, 2015, sec. America, https://www.npr.org/sections/thetwo-way/2015/10/08/446862121/oklahoma-used-the-wrong-drug-to-execute-charles-warner; Mahita

Gajanan, "Oklahoma Used Wrong Drug in Charles Warner's Execution, Autopsy Report Says," *The Guardian*, October 8, 2015, sec. US news, https://www.theguardian.com/us-news/2015/oct/08/oklahoma-wrong-drug-execution-charles-warner.

64. "Execution by Lethal Injection Procedures" (Florida Department of Corrections, 2021).

65. Mitch Smith, "Fentanyl Used to Execute Nebraska Inmate, in a First for U.S.," *New York Times*, August 14, 2018, https://www.nytimes.com/2018/08/14/us/carey-dean-moore-nebraska-execution-fentanyl.html.

66. Paul Hammel, "Witnesses Say It Appears Nebraska's First Execution in 21 Years Went Smoothly," *Omaha World-Herald*, August 15, 2018, https://omaha.com/news/crime/witnesses-say-it-appears-nebraskas-first-execution-in-21-years-went-smoothly/article_b69oda09-b716-5eaa-9eda-fa1effcad32c.html.

67. The true number is likely higher due to untraceable differences in analogous second and third drugs.

CHAPTER 4

1. In that time, Virginia electrocuted two people, Utah shot one, and Tennessee electrocuted five for a total of 343 executions.

2. Austin Sarat et al., *Gruesome Spectacles: Botched Executions and America's Death Penalty* (Stanford, CA: Stanford University Press, 2014).

3. To find mishaps, we conducted a thorough examination of every execution attempt from 2010 to 2020. First, we used the Death Penalty Information Center's execution database to build a list of every execution in the United States over those years. Then, we compiled multiple firsthand news articles about each execution. Since court filings often contain more detailed information about specific executions, we used state and federal court documents to augment our database. We

then developed a coding system to standardize how we would classify events in each execution. For example, to identify "sudden respiration," we looked for the keywords "gasping," "snorting," "coughing." "sputtering," "grunting," "blowing," and "choking" in the documents. Another researcher did a blind recoding of every execution to ensure accuracy. We further augmented the Death Penalty Information Center's database with the drugs used in each execution. "Execution Database" (Death Penalty Information Center, January 16, 2021), https://deathpenaltyinfo.org/executions/execution-database.

4. Jeffrey E. Stern, "The Cruel and Unusual Execution of Clayton Lockett," *The Atlantic*, June 2015, https://www.theatlantic.com/magazine/archive/2015/06/execution-clayton-lockett/392069/; Sean Murphy, "Oklahoma Took 51 Minutes to Find Vein in Execution," *Associated Press*, May 2, 2014.

5. Ziva Branstetter, "Death Row Inmate Killed Teen Because She Wouldn't Back Down," *Tulsa World*, April 20, 2014, https://tulsaworld.com/news/local/crime-and-courts/death-row-inmate-killed-teen-because-she-wouldnt-back-down/article_e459564b-5c60-5145-a1ce-bbd17a14417b.html.

6. Jaime Fuller, "Why Were the Two Inmates in Oklahoma on Death Row in the First Place?," *Washington Post*, April 30, 2014, https://www.washingtonpost.com/news/post-nation/wp/2014/04/30/why-were-the-two-inmates-in-oklahoma-on-death-row-in-the-first-place/.

7. Ibid.

8. Guards had to use a Taser on Lockett to get him to leave his cell that morning.

9. Stern, "The Cruel and Unusual Execution of Clayton Lockett."

10. The invasive surgery, in which officials place a central venous line by cutting away the inmate's flesh, has fallen out of favor in the medical community. Most central lines are placed

today via the Seldinger technique, a safety enhancement over the previous "cut-down" technique. Ari D. Leib, Bryan S. England, and John Kiel, "Central Line," in *StatPearls* (Treasure Island, FL: StatPearls Publishing, 2021), http://www.ncbi.nlm. nih.gov/books/NBK519511/. The cut-down procedure is so gruesome that Texas (as of 2005), Delaware (as of 2011), Ohio and Oklahoma (both as of 2014) have explicitly forbidden it in their executions.

11. Ibid.

12. Ed Pilkington, "Clayton Lockett Didn't Die of Heart Attack, Oklahoma Official Autopsy Shows," *The Guardian*, August 28, 2014, https://www.theguardian.com/world/2014/ aug/28/clayton-lockett-official-autopsy-released.

13. Stern, "The Cruel and Unusual Execution of Clayton Lockett."

14. "Execution of Clayton Lockett," *Pageviews Analysis*, accessed October 29, 2021, https://pageviews.toolforge.org/ ?project=en.wikipedia.org&range=this-year&pages=Execution _of_Clayton_Lockett.

15. Quoted in Elizabeth Weil, "The Needle and the Damage Done," *New York Times* February 11, 2017, https://www.nytimes .com/2007/02/11/magazine/11injection.t.html?pagewanted =3&_r=0

16. Ibid.

17. Stephanie Mencimer, "State Executioners: Untrained, Incompetent, and 'Complete Idiots,'" *Mother Jones* (May 7, 2014), https://www.motherjones.com/politics/2014/05/death -penalty-lethal-injections-untrained-doctors/

18. Weil, "The Needle and the Damage Done."

19. Marty Schladen, "After Four Unsuccessful Needle Pokes, Columbus Killer's Execution Called Off," *Columbus Dispatch*, November 15, 2017, https://www.dispatch.com/news/20171115/ after-four-unsuccessful-needle-pokes-columbus-killers-execution -called-off.

20. Jolie McCullough, "Texas Executes Houston Serial Killer Anthony Shore," *Texas Tribune*, January 18, 2018, https:// www.texastribune.org/2018/01/18/texas-nations-first-execution-year-set-houston-serial-killer/; Ed Pilkington, "Texas to Execute Third Prisoner This Year amid Reports of Botched Killings," *The Guardian*, February 1, 2018, sec. US news, http:// www.theguardian.com/us-news/2018/feb/01/texas-to-execute -third-prisoner-this-year-amid-reports-of-botched-killings.

21. Michael Graczyk, "'Tourniquet Killer' Executed in Texas for 1992 Strangling," *Associated Press*, January 19, 2018, https:// apnews.com/article/bd1b3d2b064f48d5a4cf3c4c5df47357.

22. Lawyers have called upon medical experts to explain the phenomenon during litigation. In Ohio's long-running lethal injection case, a federal district court received hundreds of pages of testimony from doctors and pharmacists about the effects of midazolam. As one doctor in that case remarked, "Midazolam itself is highly acidic, and while that is not problematic when the drug is used in therapeutic doses, at the dosage used in the protocol, it may cause severe burning pain upon injection." Another doctor, this time called by the state, disagreed and argued that midazolam could not cause a burning sensation, even in high doses. Ultimately, the court ruled that it was "certain or very likely that... midazolam cannot reduce consciousness to the level at which a condemned inmate will not experience severe pain." *In re Ohio Execution Protocol Litig.*, 994 F. Supp. 2d 906 (S.D. Ohio 2014). Though an appeals court later reversed the trial court's ruling, the kind of mishap that occurred in Shore's execution—inmates reporting pain during their executions—is central to many legal challenges to lethal injection.

23. "Operating Procedure 460: Execution Manual" (Virginia Department of Corrections, April 1, 2011).

24. Robert Patton, "Execution Procedures" (Oklahoma Department of Corrections, June 30, 2015).

25. Even before such dosage increases, lethal injection protocols already called for dosages far beyond what doctors had ever used therapeutically. Dosage increases have made it harder to evaluate and understand the effects of these drugs. Outside of America's execution chambers, no one has studied what happens inside a body when you inject it with 500 milligrams of midazolam.

26. Joshua Sharpe, "Convicted Killer Executed," *Atlanta Journal-Constitution*, June 21, 2019.

27. "Texas Executes 'Lovers' Lane Killer," Who Has Maintained Innocence since 2003 Slaying," *CBS News*, May 16, 2018.

28. "Texas Executes Danny Paul Bible for 1979 Rape, Murder in Houston," *CBS News*, June 27, 2018.

29. "Christopher Young, Death Row Inmate from San Antonio, Executed for Deadly 2004 Robbery," *ABC 13 Eyewitness News*, July 17, 2018.

30. Lindsey Bever, "'Murderers! Murderers!': A Convicted Killer's Last Words as He Was Executed in Florida; Eric Scott Branch Was Put to Death Thursday for the 1993 Rape and Murder of 21-Year-Old Florida College Student Susan Morris," *Washington Post*, February 23, 2018.

31. Marty Schladen, "Convicted Killer Dies by Lethal Injection," *Akron Beacon Journal*, July 19, 2018.

32. Juan A. Lozano, "Texas Executes Convicted Killer of Elderly Couple," *Associated Press*, October 22, 2010.

33. Liliana Segura, "One Night, Two Executions, and More Questions about Torture," *The Intercept*, May 25, 2019, https://theintercept.com/2019/05/25/executions-tennessee-alabama-midazolam/.

34. Ibid.

35. Ibid.

36. Steven Hale, "Tennessee Executes Billy Ray Irick for 1985 Rape and Murder," *Nashville Scene*, August 9, 2018, https://

www.nashvillescene.com/news/pithinthewind/tennessee-executes
-billy-ray-irick-for-1985-rape-and-murder/article_ca4cc482
-cb39-5818-8665-a3481517ce47.html.

37. Steven Hale, "The Execution of Billy Ray Irick," *Nashville Scene*, August 10, 2018, https://www.nashvillescene.com/
news/pithinthewind/the-execution-of-billy-ray-irick/article_
ef6c718d-bc1c-550f-926c-e68eb7fd9891.html.

38. Adam Tamburin et al., "Billy Ray Irick Execution Brings
No Resolution to Lethal Injection Debate," *The Tennessean*,
August 10, 2018.

39. Steven Hale, "Medical Expert: Billy Ray Irick Was Tortured during Execution," *Nashville Scene*, September 7, 2018,
https://www.nashvillescene.com/news/pithinthewind/medical
-expert-billy-ray-irick-was-tortured-during-execution/article
_1c31a651-5ffc-5be2-a39e-6a35f41c5558.html.

40. Adam Tamburin, "Court Blocks Autopsy for Executed
Inmate Billy Ray Irick, Citing His Religious Beliefs," *The Tennessean*, August 15, 2018, https://www.tennessean.com/story/
news/crime/2018/08/15/billy-ray-irick-execution-court-blocks
-autopsy/999087002/.

41. "Killer Provides No Comfort at Execution," *Norwalk
Reflector*, July 26, 2010.

42. Michael Auslen, "Man Executed by Lethal Injection for
1985 Slayings," *Tampa Bay Times*, October 30, 2015.

43. Jason Dearen, "Florida Executes Man Convicted of Killing 4," *South Florida Sun-Sentinel*, October 30, 2015.

44. Auslen, "Man Executed by Lethal Injection for 1985
Slayings."

45. Because this execution occurred after 2020, we do not
include it in our statistics.

46. "Oklahoma Resumes Executions; Inmate Put to Death
for 1998 Slaying," *Washington Post*, October 28, 2021.

47. Ibid.

48. Rick Cleveland, "24 Years Far Too Long for a Resolution," *Clarion Ledger*, May 20, 2010.

49. Paul Hammel, "Witnesses Say It Appears Nebraska's First Execution in 21 Years Went Smoothly," *Omaha World-Herald*, August 15, 2018, https://omaha.com/news/crime/witnesses-say-it-appears-nebraskas-first-execution-in-21-years-went-smoothly/article_b690da09-b716-5eaa-9eda-fa1effcad32c.html.

50. David R. Dow, "The Beginning of the End of America's Death-Penalty Experiment," *Politico Magazine*, July 25, 2014, https://www.politico.com/magazine/story/2014/07/the-beginning-of-the-end-of-americas-death-penalty-experiment-109394.

51. Many court cases that involve midazolam contain disagreement among medical experts. Examples include *Henness (In re Ohio Execution Protocol Litig.)*, No. 2:11-cv-1016, 2019 U.S. Dist. LEXIS 8200 (S.D. Ohio 2019) and *Glossip v. Gross*, 135 S.Ct. 2726 (2015).

52. Sarat et al., *Gruesome Spectacles*, 120.

53. This study is a source of some controversy in the medical community. A few months after it came out in *The Lancet*, the journal published two letters contradicting it and one that said it was troubling but required further assessment. See https://doi.org/10.1016/S0140-6736(05)67410-7, https://doi.org/10.1016/S0140-6736(05)67411-9, and https://doi.org/10.1016/S0140-6736(05)67412-0.

54. Alison Motluk, "Execution by Injection Far from Painless," *New Scientist*, April 14, 2005, https://www.newscientist.com/article/dn7269-execution-by-injection-far-from-painless/.

55. Ibid.

56. Noah Caldwell, Ailsa Chang, and Jolie Myers, "Gasping for Air: Autopsies Reveal Troubling Effects of Lethal Injection," *NPR*, September 21, 2020, https://www.npr.org/2020/09/21/793177589/gasping-for-air-autopsies-reveal-troubling-effects-of-lethal-injection.

57. Frank Green and Ali Rockett, "Gray Put to Death Harvey Girls' Murder," *Free Lance-Star*, January 19, 2017.

58. Gary A. Harki, "What It Was like to Watch Ricky Gray Be Put to Death," *Virginian-Pilot*, January 21, 2017, https:// www.pilotonline.com/news/article_ca41febd-32ee-5c12-8bb5 -4a32d1bae38e.html.

59. Frank Green, "Pathologist Says Ricky Gray's Autopsy Suggests Problems with Virginia's Execution Procedure," *Richmond Times-Dispatch*, July 7, 2017.

60. *Henness (In re Ohio Execution Protocol Litig.)*, 2019 U.S. Dist. LEXIS 8200.

61. *Glossip*, 135 S.Ct. 2726.

62. While newspapers and witnesses rarely have access to the administrative documents that govern executions, they often can identify when something seems to have gone wrong. As such, we counted executions in this category when journalists mentioned something out of the ordinary in addition to when they used the word "botched" itself. The rate was a slight increase from the period 1980 through 2010 when Sarat et al. found that 7.1 percent of lethal injections were botched. *Gruesome Spectacles*.

63. "Botched Executions," *Death Penalty Information Center*, accessed October 29, 2021, https://deathpenaltyinfo.org/ executions/botched-executions.

64. We found that executions between 2010 and 2020 which used a barbiturate combination lasted 10.4 minutes on average, barbiturate overdoses lasted 16.8 minutes, and sedative combinations lasted 20.7 minutes.

65. David Garland, *Peculiar Institution: America's Death Penalty in an Age of Abolition* (Cambridge, MA: Harvard University Press, 2010), 53.

66. Rick Rojas, "Why This Inmate Chose the Electric Chair over Lethal Injection," *New York Times*, February 19, 2020, sec. U.S., https://www.nytimes.com/2020/02/19/us/electric-chair -tennessee.html.

67. Brian Haas, "Tenn. Inmates Sue to Stop Electric Chair 'Torture,'" *USA Today*, August 22, 2014, https://www.usatoday .com/story/news/nation/2014/08/22/tenn-death-row-inmates -sue-to-stop-electric-chair-torture/14470995/.

68. "Killer's Electrocution Takes 17 Minutes in Indiana Chair," *Washington Post*, October 17, 1985, https://www.wash ingtonpost.com/archive/politics/1985/10/17/killers-electrocution -takes-17-minutes-in-indiana-chair/3fd99ef4-8e72-4ab3-b35a -9f7635b17267/.

69. In fact, in the May 2021 execution of Quintin Jones for the murder of his elderly great-aunt, officials in Texas did not admit witnesses into the viewing room at all, apparently mistakenly. This was a historic misstep in the era of modern capital punishment. The Associated Press reported that since 1982, when Texas executions resumed after the death penalty was reinstated nationwide, all 570 state executions were witnessed by at least one media representative. "We apologize for this critical error," said Texas Department of Criminal Justice Spokesperson Jeremy Desel. "The agency is investigating to determine exactly what occurred to ensure it does not happen again." Jolie McCullough, "For the First Time in More than 40 Years, Media Were Not Allowed to Witness a Texas Execution," *Texas Tribune*, May 20, 2021, https://www.texastribune.org/2021/05/20/texas -quintin-jones-execution-media/.

CHAPTER 5

1. Jody Lyneé Madeira, "The Ghosts in the 'Machinery of Death': The Rhetoric of Mistake in Lethal Injection Reform," in *Law's Mistakes*, ed. Austin Sarat, Lawrence Douglas, and Martha Umphrey (University of Massachusetts Press, 2016), 104, http://www.jstor.org/stable/j.ctt1hd1938.8.

2. "Gallup Poll: Public Support for the Death Penalty Lowest in a Half-Century," *Death Penalty Information Center*, Novem-

ber 24, 2020, https://deathpenaltyinfo.org/news/gallup-poll
-public-support-for-the-death-penalty-lowest-in-a-half-century.

3. We investigated protocol changes throughout the decade
by collecting protocols through Freedom of Information Act
requests filed with the departments of corrections in all states
that had the death penalty within the studied time period. Some
states (including Delaware, Louisiana, South Carolina, and
Wyoming) denied these requests, and most states provided protocols with some information redacted. To supplement our protocol database, we contacted Assistant Federal Public Defender
Jennifer Moreno, who provided us with many protocols. Moreno
formerly worked at the Berkeley Law School Lethal Injection
Project. The claims we make are limited in scope because secrecy
measures restrict our ability to create an exhaustive database. In
this section, when we claim that a particular number of states
changed their protocol in a particular way, we mean that at least
that number of states did so; other states whose protocols we
could not obtain may have as well.

4. These states are Arizona, Delaware, Idaho, Oklahoma,
Pennsylvania, South Dakota, Tennessee, Utah, and Virginia.

5. "Operating Procedure 460: Execution Manual" (Virginia
Department of Corrections, October 1, 2010).

6. "Operating Procedure 460: Execution Manual" (Virginia
Department of Corrections, July 24, 2012).

7. "Operating Procedure 460: Execution Manual" (Virginia
Department of Corrections, February 14, 2014).

8. In 2010, Virginia's first drug was sodium thiopental. In 2012,
its first drug was pentobarbital. In 2014, Virginia permitted the
first drug to be sodium thiopental, pentobarbital, or midazolam;
regardless of the drug, it prescribed a two-minute waiting period.

9. "Execution Procedures" (Idaho Department of Correc-
tion, January 6, 2012), 135.02.01.001; "JTVCC Procedure 2.7—
Execution Procedure" (Delaware Department of Correction,
May 5, 2011).

10. Robert Patton, "Execution Procedures" (Oklahoma Department of Corrections, June 30, 2015).

11. "Administration of the Death Penalty—Lethal Injection" (California Department of Corrections and Rehabilitation, January 29, 2018).

12. "JTVCC Procedure 2.7—Execution Procedure."

13. "ERM A.12(B) Capital Punishment Final Days Procedures" (South Dakota State Penitentiary, October 13, 2011).

14. "TMF 01" (Utah Department of Corrections, June 10, 2010).

15. "501 KAR 16:290. Preliminary and Post-Execution Procedures Concerning Condemned Person" (Kentucky Department of Corrections, January 12, 2018).

16. "Execution" (State of Ohio Department of Rehabilitation and Correction, October 7, 2016), ORC 2949.22, 2949.25.

17. "501 KAR 16:290. Preliminary and Post-Execution Procedures Concerning Condemned Person."

18. These states are Alabama, California, Idaho, Oklahoma, Pennsylvania, South Dakota, and Virginia.

19. "Capital Case Administration" (Commonwealth of Pennsylvania Department of Corrections, August 28, 2012). In August 2013, Missouri added a provision for medical personnel to "use standard clinical techniques to assess consciousness, such as checking for movement, opened eyes, eyelash reflex, [and] pupillary responses or diameters." "Preparation and Administration of Chemicals for Lethal Injection" (Missouri Department of Corrections, August 1, 2013). Some states specify that officials should use an electroencephalogram, which monitors brain activity, or other medical technology to access inmates' consciousness.

20. Robert Patton, "Execution Procedures" (Oklahoma Department of Corrections, September 30, 2014).

21. Malcolm Gay, "Numb and Number," *Riverfront Times*, October 12, 2005, https://www.riverfronttimes.com/stlouis/numb-and-number/Content?oid=2457308.

22. These states are Arkansas, Delaware, Florida, Idaho, Kentucky, Louisiana, Oklahoma, and South Dakota.

23. These states are Alabama, Arizona, Georgia, Indiana, Missouri, Nebraska, Nevada, North Carolina, Pennsylvania, Texas, Utah, Virginia, and Washington.

24. These states are Alabama, Florida, Indiana, and Oklahoma.

25. These states are Idaho, Kentucky, Louisiana, and Mississippi.

26. "Execution" (State of Ohio Department of Rehabilitation and Correction, January 8, 2004), ORC 2949 22.

27. "Execution" (State of Ohio Department of Rehabilitation and Correction, May 14, 2009), ORC 2949.22.

28. These states are Alabama, Arizona, Arkansas, California, Florida, Georgia, Idaho, Kentucky, Missouri, Nebraska, Ohio, Oklahoma, Tennessee, and Virginia.

29. "Department Order 710 Execution Procedures" (Arizona Department of Corrections, October 23, 2015).

30. "Execution Procedures."

31. Madeira, "The Ghosts in the 'Machinery of Death'," 84.

32. Ibid., 98.

33. To shield compounding pharmacies from public pressure to stop supplying lethal injection drugs, many states have enacted secrecy statutes to conceal the pharmacies they use. Barri Dean, "What Are Those Ingredients You Are Mixing Up behind Your Veil," *Howard Law Journal* 62, no. 1 (2018): 319.

34. Robin Konrad, "Behind the Curtain: Secrecy and the Death Penalty in the United States" (Death Penalty Information Center, November 20, 2018).

35. Corinna Barrett Lain, "Death Penalty Exceptionalism and Administrative Law," *Belmont Law Review* 8, no. 2 (2020): 578.

36. Madeira, "The Ghosts in the 'Machinery of Death'," 84.

37. "The Latest: Shade Drawn over Execution Viewing Window," *Associated Press*, August 14, 2018, https://apnews.com/article/ecda1710124740e68adaa8ede9a5222c.

38. "Nebraska Executes Carey Dean Moore in First Execution in 21 Years," *Death Penalty Information Center*, August 14, 2018, https://deathpenaltyinfo.org/news/nebraska-executes-carey-dean-moore-in-first-execution-in-21-years.

39. "Virginia Changes Execution Protocol," *WHSV 3*, March 17, 2017, https://www.whsv.com/content/news/Virginia-changes-execution-protocol-416436873.html.

40. "Plaintiffs' Brief in Opposition to Defendant's Motion to Dismiss the Complaint in BH Media Group v. Clarke" (E.D. Virg., October 30, 2019).

41. Ibid., 1.

42. This suit was pending in 2022 as this book went to press. See "Lawsuits in Arizona and Virginia Highlight Media Efforts to Witness Executions in Their Entirety," *Death Penalty Information Center*, September 24, 2019, https://deathpenaltyinfo.org/news/lawsuits-in-arizona-and-virginia-highlight-media-efforts-to-witness-executions-in-their-entirety.

43. "Arizona's Two-Hour Execution of Joseph Wood Set to Stir Debate," *NBC News*, July 24, 2014, https://www.nbcnews.com/storyline/lethal-injection/arizonas-two-hour-execution-joseph-wood-set-stir-debate-n163741.

44. Deborah W. Denno, "The Lethal Injection Quandary: How Medicine Has Dismantled the Death Penalty," *Fordham Law Review* 76, no. 1 (2007): 95.

45. Kelly A. Mennemeier, "A Right to Know How You'll Die: A First Amendment Challenge to State Secrecy Statutes Regarding Lethal Injection Drugs," *Journal of Criminal Law and Criminology* 107, no. 3 (2017): 461.

46. Konrad, "Behind the Curtain, 7.

47. "Execution," October 7, 2016.

48. *West v. Schofield*, 519 S.W. 3d 550 (Tenn. 2017).

49. Ibid., at 567.

50. "Texas Man Who Killed Neighbor Couple Has Been Executed," *Chicago Tribune*, October 5, 2016.

51. Mayra Cuevas, "Two-Hour Execution Followed Correct Protocol, Says Independent Report," *CNN*, December 22, 2014.

52. In 2011, Delaware also allowed one hour and in 2014, Louisiana allowed one hour. "JTVCC Procedure 2.7—Execution Procedure"; "Department Regulation No. C-03-001" (State of Louisiana Department of Public Safety and Corrections, March 12, 2014).

53. "Execution," October 7, 2016.

54. David M. Reutter, "Alabama Prisoner in Failed Execution Attempt Will Not Face Another," *Prison Legal News*, December 5, 2018, https://www.prisonlegalnews.org/news/2018/dec/5/alabama-prisoner-failed-execution-attempt-will-not-face-another/.

55. The others were Romell Broom, who survived a botched execution in Ohio in 2009, and Alva Campbell, whose experience we discuss in chapter 4. A third person, Willie Francis, survived a 1946 botched electrocution in Louisiana.

56. Jon Herskovitz, "Alabama's Aborted Execution Was Botched and Bloody—Lawyer," *Reuters*, February 25, 2018, sec. U.S. News, https://www.reuters.com/article/us-alabama-execution-idUSKCN1G90Y2.

57. "Notice of Submission of Expert Report of Dr. Mark Heath Re. Examination of Petitioner Doyle Hamm on February 25, 2018 in Hamm v. Dunn" (N.D. Ala., March 5, 2018).

58. The nineteen states are Alabama, Arkansas, California, Delaware, Florida, Georgia, Idaho, Kentucky, Missouri, Nebraska, North Carolina, Ohio, Oklahoma, South Dakota, Tennessee, Texas, Utah, Virginia, and Washington.

59. "Why Execution Drugs Don't Always Work As Expected," *HuffPost*, May 1, 2014, sec. Science, https://www.huffpost.com/entry/why-lethal-injection-drugs-dont-always-work_n_5246031.

60. The thirteen states are Alabama, Arkansas, Florida, Georgia, Idaho, Missouri, Nebraska, North Carolina, Ohio, Tennessee, Texas, Virginia, and Washington.

61. Patton, "Execution Procedures," June 30, 2015.

62. These states are Arizona, California, Delaware, Idaho, Indiana, Kentucky, Louisiana, Mississippi, Ohio, Oklahoma, Pennsylvania, South Dakota, Virginia, and Washington.

63. "Execution Procedures."

64. "Capital Punishment Procedures" (Mississippi Department of Corrections, July 28, 2015).

65. "Execution Protocol" (Nebraska Department of Correctional Services, January 26, 2017).

66. Eric Berger, "The Executioners' Dilemmas," *University of Richmond Law Review* 49 (2015), 748.

67. Lain, "Death Penalty Exceptionalism and Administrative Law," 554.

68. Ibid.

69. Kelsey Davis, "Ronald Smith Executed for 1994 Capital Murder," *Montgomery Advertiser*, December 8, 2016.

70. Kent Faulk, "Death Row Inmate Ronald Bert Smith Has Been Executed," *AL.com*, December 8, 2016, sec. Birmingham Real-Time News, https://www.al.com/news/birmingham/2016/12/alabama_death_row_inmate_is_se.html.

71. Ibid.

72. Deborah Denno, "When Legislatures Delegate Death: The Troubling Paradox Behind State Uses of Electrocution and Lethal Injection and What It Says about Us," *Ohio State University Law Journal* 63 (2002), https://ir.lawnet.fordham.edu/faculty_scholarship/118/.

73. "Execution" (State of Ohio Department of Rehabilitation and Correction, November 21, 2001).

74. "Execution," October 7, 2016.

75. "Execution," January 8, 2004.

76. "Execution" (State of Ohio Department of Rehabilitation and Correction, July 10, 2006), ORC 2949 22.

77. "Execution" (State of Ohio Department of Rehabilitation and Correction, October 11, 2006), ORC 2949 22.

78. "Execution," May 14, 2009.

79. "Execution" (State of Ohio Department of Rehabilitation and Correction, November 30, 2009), ORC 2949.22, 2949.25.

80. "Method of Execution of Death Sentence," ORC Ann. § 2949.22 (2001).

81. "Execution" (State of Ohio Department of Rehabilitation and Correction, March 9, 2011), ORC 2949.22, 2949.25.

82. "Execution" (State of Ohio Department of Rehabilitation and Correction, April 11, 2011), ORC 2949.22, 2949.25.

83. "Ohio Executes Man for Beating, Stomping Fellow Inmate to Death in Cincinnati," *Cleveland.com*, April 12, 2011, https://www.cleveland.com/metro/2011/04/ohio_executes_man _for_beating.html.

84. "Execution" (State of Ohio Department of Rehabilitation and Correction, September 18, 2011), ORC 2949.22, 2949.25.

85. Kantele Franko, "East Cleveland Man Who Killed 3 Sleeping Sons," *News-Herald*, November 16, 2011.

86. Andrew Welsh-Huggins, "Ohio Prepares to Execute 1st Inmate in 6 Months," *Associated Press*, April 18, 2012.

87. "Execution" (State of Ohio Department of Rehabilitation and Correction, October 10, 2013), ORC 2949.22, 2949.25.

88. Intramuscular injections are like a flu shot: a relatively quick injection into muscle rather than a vein. Intravenous injections require setting an IV line, but intramuscular injections do not.

89. See Amicus Brief filed with the United States Supreme Court in the case of *Nance v. Ward*, October 22, 2021. https:// www.supremecourt.gov/DocketPDF/21/21-439/197455/20211025 135406218_21-439%20Motion%20for%20Leave%20to%20 File%20Amicus%20Brief.pdf

90. Berger, "The Executioners' Dilemmas," 739–40.

CHAPTER 6

1. In the eighteenth century, this secrecy took the form of hoods placed over the inmate's head to hide their contortions. With the advent of the electric chair in 1890, it took the form of midnight executions conducted deep behind the walls of state prisons. Richard C. Dieter, "Methods of Execution and Their Effect on the Use of the Death Penalty in the United States Symposium: The Lethal Injection Debate: Law and Science," *Fordham Urban Law Journal* 35, no. 4 (2008): 791.

2. According to S. E. Smith, states tend to implement "minor reforms" after botches. "Going through All These Things Twice: A Brief History of Botched Executions," *Otago Law Review* 12, no. 4 (2009): 777–828.

3. Deborah W. Denno, "The Lethal Injection Quandary: How Medicine Has Dismantled the Death Penalty," *Fordham Law Review* 76, no. 1 (2007): 117.

4. This assertion is supported by scholars like Madeira. Madeira states that "rapid innovation also intensifies organizational stress, increasing the likelihood of the very mistakes that reforms purportedly reduce," and as a result, "capital punishment by lethal injection is characterized by frequent reform and, as a result, has become engulfed in a 'culture of mistake.'" "The Ghosts in the 'Machinery of Death': The Rhetoric of Mistake in Lethal Injection Reform," in *Law's Mistakes*, ed. Austin Sarat, Lawrence Douglas, and Martha Umphrey, 83–84 (University of Massachusetts Press, 2016), http://www.jstor.org/stable/j.ctt1hd1938.8.

5. James C. Feldman, "Nothing Less Than the Dignity of Man: The Eighth Amendment and State Efforts to Reinstitute Traditional Methods of Execution," *Washington Law Review* 90, no. 3 (2015): 1330–36; Maurice Chammah, Andrew Cohen, and Eli Hagar, "After Lethal Injection," *The Marshall Project*, June 1, 2015, https://www.themarshallproject.org/2015/06/01/

after-lethal-injection. See also "Manner of Federal Executions," *Federal Register* (December 1, 2020), https://www.federalregister .gov/documents/2020/12/01/C1-2020-25867/manner-of-federal -executions.

6. Joseph Choi, "DeWine Says Lethal Injection 'Impossible' Option for Ohio Executions," *The Hill*, December 8, 2020, https://thehill.com/homenews/state-watch/529306-dewine -says-lethal-injection-impossible-option-for-ohio-executions.

7. "Ohio Governor Mike DeWine Calls Lethal Injection a Practical Impossibility, Says State Will Not Execute Anyone in 2021," *Death Penalty Information Center*, December 15, 2020, https://deathpenaltyinfo.org/news/ohio-governor-mike-dewine -calls-lethal-injection-a-practical-impossibility-says-state-will -not-execute-anyone-in-2021.

8. We are grateful to two anonymous reviewers of an earlier version of this book for highlighting these points.

9. These narratives play a key role in Supreme Court decisions on methods of execution. See, for example, *Baze v. Rees* 553 U.S. 35 (2008).

10. Austin Sarat et al., *Gruesome Spectacles: Botched Executions and America's Death Penalty* (Stanford, CA: Stanford University Press, 2014), 7; David Garland, *Peculiar Institution: America's Death Penalty in an Age of Abolition* (Cambridge, MA: Belknap Press of Harvard University Press, 2010), 183.

11. Dieter, "Methods of Execution and Their Effect on the Use of the Death Penalty in the United States Symposium," 798.

12. *Arthur v. Dunn*, 580 U.S. _____ (2017), 137 S.Ct. 725 (2017), Sotomayor dissenting, https://www.supremecourt.gov/ orders/courtorders/022117zor_0759.pdf.